Charles Godfrey Leland

Hans Breitmann's Barty and Other Ballads

Charles Godfrey Leland

Hans Breitmann's Barty and Other Ballads

ISBN/EAN: 9783744796583

Printed in Europe, USA, Canada, Australia, Japan

Cover: Foto ©Thomas Meinert / pixelio.de

More available books at **www.hansebooks.com**

HANS BREITMANN'S BARTY,

AND OTHER BALLADS.

HANS BREITMANN'S BARTY

AND OTHER BALLADS.

BY

CHARLES G. LELAND

WARD, LOCK AND CO.
LONDON : WARWICK HOUSE, SALISBURY SQUARE, E.C.
NEW YORK : BOND STREET.

INTRODUCTION.

THE model of these 'Ballads,' we suspec
was Mr. Lowell's 'Biglow Papers,' althoug
the conglomerate character of the Germar
American citizen has been so well portraye
herein, that there are few actual points c
resemblance between the two composition
The distinguishing peculiarity of both satire
seems to be this,—political shortcomings bur
lesqued, or satirized, by a comparison wit
social failings and home weaknesses : the on

kind of national shortcoming made to expound whilst ridiculing the other.

CHARLES G. LELAND, from whose pen we have the '*Breitmann Ballads*,' has long been known in the United States as the author of some admirable pieces, prose and verse, first published in newspapers and magazines, and particularly for his skill in translating from the German. If we mistake not, he is another of those Americans, who, like Bayard Taylor, Ross, and Dana, have travelled extensively in the Old World.

The hero, 'Breitmann,' is said to have been one Jost, a German trooper, of the Fifteenth Pennsylvania Volunteers Cavalry. The language employed is that broken speech used by German emigrants in the Great Republic. As there are some millions of these foreigners and their children scattered throughout the Thirty-one States (the bakery, grocery, or store for sweets and lager-beer, in almost every town, being conducted by a German), it cannot be wondered at that already the English language in America has become to some extent Germanized. Thus, all the familiar words in German speech, the questions and answers of every-day life, and the names of common objects, are as well known and recognised among all classes throughout the Union as the coins of Prussia and Austria are current and acceptable tender.

The various Americanisms and slang

expressions which Breitmann employs, or
perverts, with such ludicrous effect, will, it is
hoped, be found sufficiently explained in the
few notes which the editors have added where
they seemed desirable.

CONTENTS.

HANS BREITMANN'S* 'BARTY'

[* BREITMANN, '*broad (or huge) man,*' *has the hint
in it of a big swaggerer or burly boaster.* HANS *is the
commonest of all Christian names in Germany, being
equivalent to our* JOHN.]

H ANS BREITMANN gif a barty;
  Dey hat biano-blayin',
I fell'd in luf mit a 'Merican frau,[1]
Her name vas Madilda Yane.
She hat haar ash prown ash a pretzel,[2]

---

[1] 'Frau:' *Ger.* A wife.
[2] 'Brezel,' or 'Bretzel,' a cracknel or bun in the shape of a
letter B (or nearer still to the figure 8), flavoured with salt.

Her eyes vas himmel-plue,[1]
Und ven dey looket indo mine,
  Dey shplit mine heart in doo.

Hans Breitmann gif a barty,
  I vent dere, you'll be pound;
I valtz't mit Madilda Yane,
  Und vent shpinnen' roundt und roundt.
Der pootiest Fraulein[2] in der hause,
  She vayed 'pout doo hoondred pounat,
Und efery dime she gif a shoomp
  She make der vinders sound.

Hans Breitmann gif a barty,
  I dells you, it cosht him dear;

---

[1] 'Himmel-blau:' heavenly, or sky-blue.
  'Fraulein:' *Ger*. Young lady.

Dey rolled in more ash sefen kecks
Of foost-rate lager-peer.[1]
Und venefer dey knocks der shpicket[2] in
Der Deutschers gifs a cheer
I dinks dat so vine a barty
Nefer coom to a het[3] dis year.

Hans Breitmann gif a barty;
Dere all vash Souse undt Brouse,[4]

---

[1] 'Lager-bier:' the common German drink used in the United States, so named from improved quality being kept in a cellar or warehouse : from '*lagern*,' to store up.

[2] 'Shpicket,' *i.e.* spigot.

[3] 'Come to a head,' a simile common enough in America, drawn by the vulgar from the uncertain progress of imposthumes, and used to denote the success, or non-success, that may attend any undecided affair. In England the phrase is occasionally employed, as 'the conspiracy came to a head.'

[4] 'Saus und Braus:' *Ger.* Riot and Bustle.

Ven der sooper comed in, de gompany
Did make demselfs to house;[1]
Dey ate das Brot und Gensy-broost,[2]
Der Bratwurst und Braten vine,[3]
Undt vash der Abendessen[4] down
Mit vour parrels ov Neckarwein.[5]

Hans Breitmann gif a barty;
Ve all cot troonk ash bigs.
I poot mine mout' to a parrel of peer
Undt emptied it oop mit a schwigs;

[1] 'To house:' Americanism for 'at home.'
[2] 'Das Brot und Gensy-broost:' *Ger.* 'Das Brod und Gänsebrust' (bread and white meat of the goose, the latter cut from the breast, and cured by smoking).
[3] 'Der Bratwurst und Braten vine:' sausages and roast meats fine.
[4] 'Abendessen:' *Ger.* Supper.
[5] 'Neckarwein:' wine grown on the Neckar.

Und den I giss'd Madilda Yane
Und she schlog me on der kop,[1]
Und der gompany vighted mit daple-lecks
Dill der coonshtable mate oos shtop.

Hans Breitmann gif a barty—
Vhere ish dat barty now?
Vhere ish der lufly colden gloud
Dat float on der moundain's prow?
Vhere ish de himmelstrahlende stern[2]—
De shtar of de shpirit's light?
All gon'd afay mit der lager-peer—
Afay in de ewigkeit![3]

---

[1] 'Schlog me on der kop,' for 'Schlug mich auf den Kopf:' struck me on the head.

[2] 'Himmelstrahlende stern:' *Ger.* 'Heavenly-shining star.'

[3] 'Ewigkeit:' *Ger.* 'Eternity;' 'gone for ever.'

BREITMANN AND THE 'TURNERS.'

(THE GYMNASTIC SOCIETY.)

HANS BREITMANN choined de Turners,
  Nofember in de fall,
Und dey gif't a boostin' bender[1]
All in de Turner Hall.
Dere coomed de whole Gesangverein[2]
  Mit der Liederlich Apfel Chor,[3]

[1] 'A bursting bender,' a grand banquet: from 'to bend,' perverted into to take relaxation by indulgence in drink.
[2] Singing Society.
[3] Burlesque title of a Harmonic Society, 'The Jolly Dogs Apple-of-our-Eye Choral Society.'

Und dey blowed on de drooms und stroomed
   on de fifes
Till dey couldn't refife no more.

Hans Breitmann choined de Turners,
   Dey all set oop some shouts,
Dey took'd him into dair Turner Hall,
   Und poots him droo a course of shprouts,[1]
Dey poots him on de barell-hell pars[2]
   Und shtands him oop on his head,
Und dey poomps de peer mit an enchine hose[3]
   In his mout' dill he's 'pout half tead!

Hans Breitmann choined de Turners;
   Dey make shimnastig dricks

---

[1] A series of instructive lessons: 'Just as the twig is bent,' &c.
[2] Parallel bars.   [3] Fire-engine tubing.

He stoot on de middle of de floor,
　Und put oop a fifdy-six.[1]
Und den he drows it to de roof,
　Und schwig off a treadful trink :
De veight coom toomple pack on his headt,
　Und py shinks ! he didn't vink !

Hans Breitmann choined de Turners :—
　Mein Gott ! how dey drinked und shwore !
Dere vas Schwabians und Tyrolers,
　Und Bavarians by de score.
Some vellers coomed from de Rheinland,
　Und Frankfort-on-de-Main,
Boot dere vas only von Sharman dere,
　Und *he* vas a *Holstein Dane,*

---

[1] A fifty-six-pound weight, or dumb-bell.

Hans Breitmann choined de Turners.
  Mit a Limpurg' cheese[1] he coom;
Ven he oben de pox it schmell so loudt
  It knock de musik doomb.
Ven de Deutschers kit de vlavour,
  It coorl de haar on deir head;
Boot dere vas dwo Amerigans dere;
  Und, py tam! it kilt dem dead!

Hans Breitmann choined de Turners;
  De ladies coomed in to see;
Dey poot dem in de blace for de gals,
  All in der gal-lerie.

---

[1] Limburger cheese—an abomination guilty of the most powerful odour. A story is told in the United States of a sharp fellow taking a cellar on lease, and, by storing it with 'Limburger Käse,' compelling the landlord to buy back the long lease, all the other tenants being driven frantic.

Dey ashk : ' Vhere ish der Breitmann ?'
Und dey dremple mit awe und fear
Vhen dey see him schwingen' py de toes,
A-trinkin' lager-peer.

Hans Breitmann choined de Turners :—
I dells you vot, py tam !
Dey sings de great Urbummel-lied :[1]
De holy Sharman psalm.
Und vhen dey kits to de gorus
You ought to hear dem dramp !
It scared der Teufel down below
To hear dem Dootchmen schtamp.

Hans Breitmann choined de Turners :—
By Donner ! it vas crandt,

[1] German slang term for the loafer's hymn, or arch-lazy-
bones' song.

Ven de whole of dem goes a-valkin'
Und dancin' on deir hand,
Mit de veet all vavin' in de air,
Gottstausend !¹ vot a dricks !
Dill der Breitmann vall und dey all co town
Shoost like a row of bricks.

Hans Breitmann choined de Turners :—
Dey lay dere in a heap,
Und slept dill de early sonnen-shine
Come in at de vindow creep;
Und de preeze it vake them from deir tre^m,
Und dey go to kit deir veed :
Here hat dis song an Ende—
Das ist DAS BREITMANNSLIED.²

¹ A euphemistic German oath for 'God's Thousand Thun-
ders !'
² 'This is the *Lay* of Breitmann.'

BREITMANN IN BATTLE.

'TUNC TAPFRE AUSFUHRERE STREITUM ET RITTRI
DIGNUM POTUERE ERJAGERE LOBUM.'

DER FADER UNDT DER SON.

I DINKS I'll co a-vightin''—outshpoke
der Breitemann,
'It's eighdeen hoonderd fordy-eight since *I*
kits swordt in handt;
Dese fourdeen years mit Hecker all roostin' I
haf been,
Boot now I kicks der Teufel[1] oop and goes
for sailin' in.'[2]

'Der Teufel,' the Prince of Darkness.
[2] 'Sailing in:' American for 'going in;' equivalent to the
Cockney expression 'wiring in.'

'If you go land out-ridin',' said Caspar Pickle-
tongue,
'Foost ding you knows you cooms agross
some repels prave und young,
Avay town Sout' in Tixey, dey'll schplit you
like a clam '—[1]
'For dat,' spoke out der Breitmann, 'I doos
not gare one tam!

'Who der Teufel pe's de repels, undt vhere
dey kits dair sass,[2]
If dey make a roon on Breitmann he'll soon
let out der gas;[3]

---

[1] 'Clam,' the common American name for the round,
smooth-shelled bivalve, which can be easily opened or split
by a knife-point.

[2] Sauce.   [3] 'Gas,' American for windy words.

I 'll shplit dem like kartoffells :[1] I 'll shlog em
    on de kop ;[2]
I 'll set de plackguarts roonin' so dey von't
    know vheres to shtop.'

Und den outshpoke der Breitmann, mit his
    schlaeger[3] py his side :
' Forvarts, my pully landsmen ![4] it 's dime to
    roon undt ride ;
Vill ridin', vill vightin'—der Copitain I 'll
    pe,

[1] ' Kartoffel,' potatoes.
[2] Strike them on the head.   See note [1], p. 15.
[3] ' Schläger :' *Ger*. Sword.
[4] ' Bully landsmen,' a curious combination of American
slang and German.   Bully is equivalent to fine, brave,
powerful; as, a ' bully horse,' a ' bully man.'   Landsmann,
Ger. for fellow-countryman.

It's sporn[1] undt horn undt saddle now—all
in der Cavallrie !'

Und ash dey rode droo Vinchesder,[2] so herrlich[3] to pe seen,
Dere coom't some repel cavallrie a-ridin' on
der creen ;
Mit[4] a sassy repel Dootchman—ein colonel in
gommand :
Says he, 'Vot Teufel makes you here in dis
mein Faaderland ?

'You're dressed oop like a shentlemann mit
your plackguart Yankee grew,

---

[1] 'Sporn :' *Ger.* Spur.
[2] Winchester, where there was an action during the American civil war.
[3] 'Herrlich :' *Ger.* Gallant.   [4] 'Mit :' *Ger.* With.

You mudsills[1] und meganics! Der Teufel put
    you droo!
Old Yank, you ought to shtay at home und
    dake your liddle horn,[2]
Mit some oldt voomans for a noorse'—der
    Breitmann laugh mit shkorn.

'Und should I trink mein lager-peer und roost
    mine self to home?
I 'fe got too many dings like you to mash
    beneat' my thoom:

[1] 'Mudsill,' a term of reproach used by the Southerners
against the Northerners, meaning the sediment, or very dregs
of mud. From *mud-sill*, the timber which underlies the
'sleeper' on a railway track; figuratively applied by the
proud Southerners to poor people—or the working classes—
upon whose shoulders the upper classes repose in affluence
and security.

[2] 'Little horn,' drink; from the country people's use of
cows' horns for drinking-measures.

In many a fray und vierce foray dis Dootchman will be feared
Pefore he stops dis vightin' trade—'twas dere
he grayed his peard.'

'I pools dat peard out by de roots—I gifs
him sooch a dwist
Dill all de plood roons out, you tamn'd old
Apolitionist![1]
Your creenpacks[2] mit your swordt und vatch
right ofer you moost shell,[3]

---

[1] Abolitionist.

[2] Greenbacks: the United States bank-notes, printed on
the reverse with green non-photographable ink.

[3] 'Shell out,' to pay over; from the analogy of opening a
pocket-book to take out coin, and of opening a shell to
extract the fish.

Und den you goes to Libby[1] shtraight—und
    after dat to h–ll !'

'Mein creenpacks und mein schlaeger, I kits
    'em in New York,
To gif dem up to creenhorns,[2] young man, is
    not de talk;'
De heroes shtopped deir sassin' here und
    gross't deir sabres dwice't,
Und de vay dese Deutschers vent to vork vos
    von pig ding on ice.[3]

---

[1] Libby Prison at Richmond, for prisoners of war.
[2] Greenhorns.
[3] 'A big thing on ice.' All the restaurants in the United
States have refrigerators, in which are kept eatables likely
to be spoiled by heat in summer; hence, the rarest delicacies
are most carefully put 'on ice,' and 'a big thing' also 'on
ice, would necessarily be some exceptionably fine rarity.

Der younker fetch der oldter sooch a gottall-
    machty schmack
Der Breitmann dinks he really hears his skool
    go shplit und crack ;
Der repel shoomps dwelf paces pack, und so
    he safe his life :
Der Breitmann says : ' I guess dem shoomps
    you learns dem of your vife.'

' If I should learn of vomans I dinks it vere a
    shame,
Bei Cott I am a shendlemann, aristograt, und
    game.
My fader vos anoder—I lose him fery young—

<hr>

[1] ' God-almighty :' burlesque adverb for ' excessively,' in
connexion with a suitable adjective understood.

Der Teufel take your soul   Coom on ! I 'll
    shplit your vaggin' tongue !'

A Yankee drick der Breitmann dried—dat
    oldt gray-pearded man—
For ash de repel raised his swordt, beneat'
    dat swordt he ran.
All roundt der shlim yoong repel's vaist his
    arms oldt Breitmann pound,
Und schlinged him down oopon his pack und
    laidt him on der ground.

'Who rubs against olt kittle-pots may keep
    vite—if he can,
Say, vot you dinks of vightin' now, mit dis old
    shendlemann ?

Your dime is oop; you got to die, und I your
  briest vill pe ;
Peliev'st dou in Morál Ideas ?[1]   If so, I lets
  you free.'

'I don't know nix[2] apout ideas—no more dan
  'pout Saint Paul,
Since I 'fe peen down in Tixey[3] I kits no books
  at all ;

[1] ' Moral Ideas :' jocosely said of the extreme Abolitionists
and Unionists, who, in the midst of the most sanguinary
battles of the Civil War always roundly asserted that they
desired not to coerce, or conquer,—only to persuade by
' Moral Ideas.'

[2] ' Nichts :' *Ger*. Nothing.

[3] Dixie's Land, *i. e.* the Southern States.   Many interpret-
ations of this expression have been given, and it would be
difficult in our limited space to discuss them with any degree
of satisfaction to the reader.

I'm greener ash de clofer-grass; I'm shtupid
    ash a shpoon ;
I'm ignoranter ash de nigs[1]—for dey takes de
    Tribune.[2]

'Mein fader's name vas Breitmann, I heard
    mein mutter say,
She read de bapers dat he died after she rooned
    afay ;
Dey say he leaft some broperty—berhaps 'tvas
    all a sell—
If I could lay mein hands on it I likes it
    mighty vell.

---

[1] 'Nig' for nigger.

[2] '*Tribune,*' the New York daily paper of that name, the
organ of the extreme Abolitionists, and sarcastically stated in
the South to number amongst its subscribers a great many
self-educated niggers.

'Und vas dy fader Breitmann? *Bist du*[1] his
    kit' und kin?
Denn know dat *ich* der Breitmann dein lieber
    Vater bin?'[2]
Der Breitmann poolled his hand-shoe[3] off und
    shookt him py de handt;
'Ve'll haf some trinks on strengt' of dis—or
    else may I pe tamn'd!'

'Oh! fader, how I shlog your kop,' der
    younger Breitmann said;
'I'd den dimes sooner had it coom right down
    on mine own headt!'

[1] 'Art thou?'
[2] 'Know that I your beloved Father Breitmann am.'
[3] Handschuh: *Ger.* Glove.

C

'Oh, never mind—dat soon dry oop—I shticks
  him mit a blaster;
If I had shplit you like a fish, dat vere an
  vorse tisassder.'

Dis fight did last all afternoon—*wohl*[1] to de
  fesper-tide,[2]
Und droo de streets of Vinchesder, der Breitmann he did ride.
Vot vears der Breitmann on his hat? De
  ploom of fictory!
Who's dat a-ridin' py his side? 'Dis here's
  mein son,' says he.

---

[1] 'Wohl,' well, even unto.
[2] 'Vesper-zeit:' *Ger.* Evening, even-tide.

How stately rode der Breitmann oop!—how
    lordly he kit down!
How glorious from de great *pokal*[1] he trink de
    peer so prown!
But der Yunger bick der parrel oop und
    schwig him all at one.
'Bei Gott! *dat* settles all dis dings—I *know*
    dou art mein son!'

Der one has cot a fader; de oder foundt a
    schild.
Bofe ride oopon one war-bath now in pattle
    vierce und fild.

---

[1] 'Pokal,' drinking-cup: in this case the large glass pint
beer-mug used in America.

It makes so glad our hearts to hear dat dey
did so succeed—
Und damit hat sein Ende DES JUNGEN BREIT-
MANN'S LIED.[1]

[1] 'And here comes to its end the Lay of Breitmann
the Younger.'

BREITMANN IN MARYLAND.

D ER BREITMANN mit his gompany,
   Rode out in Marylandt.
' Dere 's nix to trink in dis countrie ;
   Mine droat 's as dry as sand.
It 's light canteen und haversack,
   I 's hoonger mixed mit doorst ;
Und if ve had some lager-peer
   I 'd trink oontil I boorst.
     Gling, glang, gloria !
   Ve 'd trink oontil ve boorst.

'Herr Leutd'nant, take a dozen men,
  Und ride dis landt around!
Herr Feldwebel,[1] go foragin'
  Dill somedings goot ish found.
Gotts-donder![2] men, go ploonder!
  Ve hafn't trinked a pit
Dis fourdeen hours! If I had peer
  I'd sauf[3] oontil I shplit!
    Gling, glang, gloria!
  Ve'd sauf oontil ve shplit!

Ad mitternacht[4] a horse's hoofs
  Goom raddlin' droo de gamp;

---

[1] 'Herr Feldwebel:' *Ger.*   Master Serjeant.
[2] 'God's Thunder:' a noisy German oath.
[3] 'Saufen:' *Ger.*   To drink, carouse.
[4] Midnight.

'Rouse dere !—coom rouse der house dere!

Herr Copitain—ve moost tromp !

Der scouds haf foundt a repel town,

Mit repel davern near,

A repel keller[1] in de cround,

Mit repel lager-peer ! !

Gling, glang, gloria !

All fool of lager-peer !'

Gottsdonnerkreuzschockschwerenoth ![2]

How Breitmann broked de bush ![3]

' O let me see dat lager-peer !

O let me at him rush !

Und is mein zabre sharp und true,

[1] Cellar.

[2] A burlesque oath, high sounding, and full of terrible meaning.

[3] Break the bush, *i.e.* rush through a thicket.

Und is mein var-horse goot ?

To get one quart of lager-peer

I 'd shpill a sea of ploot.

Gling, glang, gloria !

I 'd shpill a sea of ploot.

' Funf[1] hoonderd repels hold de down,

One hoonderd strong are ve ;

Who gares a tam for all de odds

Vhen men so dirsty pe ?'

Und in dey smashed und down dey crashed,

Like donder-polts dey fly,

Rush fort as der vild yager[2] cooms

' Fünf,' five.

[2] ' Yager,' *i. e.* jager, sharpshooter or rifleman ; from the first corps of this kind being formed of gamekeepers and hunters. ' Wild Jager,' the Wild Huntsman of German Legends.

Mit blitzen[1] droo de shky.

    Gling, glang, gloria!

Like blitzen droo de shky.

How flewed to rite, how flewed to left,

    De moundains, drees, und hedge!

How left und rite de yager-corps

    Vent donderin' droo de pridge!

Und splash und splosh dey ford de shtream

    Vere not some pridges pe:

All dripplin' in de moondlight peam

    Stracks[2] vent de cavallrie.

      Gling, glang, gloria!

Der Breitmann's cavallrie.

---

[1] 'Blitzen,' *Ger.* Lightning.
[2] 'Stracks,' stnright, direct.

Und hoory, hoory, on dey rote,

Oonheedin' vet or try ;

Und horse und rider shnort und blowed,

Und shparklin' bepples fly.

Ropp ! Ropp ! I shmell de parley-prew !

Dere 's somedings goot ish near.

Ropp ! Ropp !—I scent de kneiperei ;[1]

Ve 've cot to lager-peer !

Gling, glang, gloria !

Ve 've cot to lager-peer !

Hei ! how de carpine pullets klinged[2]

Oopon de helmets hart !

Oh, Breitmann—how dy zabre ringed ;

[1] 'Kneipe,' beerhouse.
[2] 'How the carbine bullets rang.'

Du alter Knasterbart ![1]

De contrapands[2] dey sing for choy

To see der rebs co town,

Und hear der Breitmann crimly gry :

Hoorah !—ve 've dook de down.

Gling, glang, gloria !

Victoria, victoria !

De Dootch have dook de down.

Mid shout und crash und zabre vash,

Und vild husaren[3] shout

---

[1] ' You old grumbler !' And probably a punning allusion
to the 'Nasty Boy,' the exact American equivalent to our
' Ugly Customer.'

[2] 'Contrabands.' Gen. Butler would not return fugitive
slaves to claimants, on the ground of their being useful as
workmen to the enemy, and, therefore, *contraband* of war.

[3] ' Husaren shout,' cheering like hussars.

De Dootchmen boorst de keller in,
    Und rollt der lager out;
And in the coorlin' powder shmoke,
    Vile shtill der pullets sung,
Dere shtood der Breitmann, axe in hand(‚
    A-knockin' out der boong.
      Gling, glang, gloria!
        Victoria! Encoria!
    De shpicket beats de boong.

Gotts! vot a shpree der Breitmann had
    Vhile yet his hand was red,
A-trinkin' lager from his poots
    Among de repel tead.
'Tvas dus dey vent at mitternight
    Along der moundain side:

'Tvas dus dey help ' make history !'[1]
Dis vas der Breitmann's ride.
Gling, glang, gloria ;
Victoria ! Victoria !
Cer'visia, encoria ?
De treadful midtnight ride
Of Breitmann's vildt Freischarlinger,[2]
All vamous, proad, und vide.

[1] One of the Northern orators said the army were 'making history' by their actions.
[2] 'Freischarlinger :' *Ger.* Freischarler, volunteers, par-tisans.

BREITMANN AS A 'BUMMER.'[1]

DER SHENERAL SHERMAN holts
   oop on his coorse,
He shtops ad de gross-road und reins in his
   horse.
' Dere 's a ford on der rifer dis day ve moost
   dake,
Or elshe de grand army in bieces shall
   preak!'

[1] ' Bummler,' an idler, a loafer.

Ven shoost ash dis vord vrom his lips hat
cone bast,
Dere coom't a young orterly gallopin' vast,
Who gry mit amazement: 'Here, Shen'ral!
Goot Lord!
*Dat Bummer der Breitmann ish holdin' der
ford!'*

Der Shen'ral he ootered no hymn und no
psalm,
But opened his lips und he priefly say,
'D——n!'[1]
Dere moost hafe been viskey on dat side der
rifer;
To get it dose shaps vould set hell in a
shiver;

[1] 'Our army swore terribly in Flanders.'

But now dat dey holdt it, ride quick to deir
    aid :
Ho, Sickles ![1] moof promp'ly, sendt town a
    prigate !
Dat Dootchman moost vork mighty hardt mit
    ish sword
If againsd a whole army he holdt to de ford.'

Dey spoored on, dey hoory'd on, gallopin'
    shtraight,
But vor Breitmann help coomed shoost a
    liddle too late,
Vor as de Lauwine[2] goes smash mit her pound,
So on to de Bummers de repels coom down :

[1] General Sickles, who redeemed an injured reputation
for shooting his wife's seducer, by losing a leg during the
war.
[2] 'Lauwine :' *Ger*. Avalanche.

Heinrich von Schinkenstein's tead in de road,
Dieterich Hinkelbein's flat as a toad ;
Und Sepperl—Tyroler—shpoke nefer a vordt,
But shoost '*Mutter Gottes !*'[1] und died in de
ford.

Itsch'l of Innspruck ish drilled droo de hair
Einer aus Bœblingen — he, doo, vash dere—
Karl of Karlsruh is shot near de fence,
(His horse vash o'erloadet mit toorkies und
hens,)
Und dough he like a ravin' mad cannibal
vought,
Yet der Breitmann—der capt'n—der hero—
vash gaught ;

----

[1] 'Holy Virgin,' 'God's Mother !'

Und de last dings ve saw, he vas died mit a
    gord,
Vor de repels hat goppled him oop[1] at de
    vord.

Dey shtripped off his goat und skyugled[2] his
    poots,
Dey dressed him mit rags of a repel re-
    cruits;
But von gray-haared oldt veller shmiled crimly
    und bet
Dat Breitmann vouldt pe a pad egg for dem
    yet.

[1] 'To gobble up,' to capture a whole party, all to a man,
as a hungry turkey swallows a cropful of grains at a gulp.
[2] 'Skyugle,' a burlesque Americanism, implying some act
too horrible to express plainly. Here 'they made away with
his boots.'

'He has more on ish pipe ash dem vellers
    allows;
He has cardts yet in hand und *das Spiel ist
    nicht aus*,[1]
Dey'll find dat dey dook in der Teufel to
    poard,[2]
De day dey pooled Breitmann vell ofer de
    ford.

In de Bowery[3] each bier-haus mit crape vas
    oopdone,
Vhen dey read in de babers dat Breitmann
    vas cone;

[1] 'The game is not yet played out.'

[2] Took in the Devil to board and lodge. 'To take into
board' is a very common phrase in America, where one-half
of the people 'board' at other people's houses or hotels.

[3] The Bowery is a large street in New York, abounding in
places of resort for Germans; as dance-houses, bier-gartens,
the German Theatre, &c.

Und der Dootch all cot troonk oopon lager
    und wein,

At de great Trauer-fest[1] of de Turner-
    Verein.[2]

Dere vas wein-en mit weinen[3] ven beoplesh
    did dink

Dat Sherman's great Sharman cood nefer
    more trink.

Und in Villiam Shtreet[4] veepin' und vailen'
    vas hoor'd,

Pecause der Hans Breitmann vas lost at de
    ford.

[1] Mourning-celebration.

[2] The Germans imported their Gymnastic Society into the United States, keeping the same name, derived from 'tur-nen,' to tilt or joust, but popularly supposed to mean 'to turn,' as in acrobatic feats. The members are known as 'Turners.'

[3] 'Whining with wine-ing :' *i.e.* crying and drinking.

[4] William Street, New York, is full of German drinking-places.

SECOND PART.

*I*N *dulce jubilo* now ve all sings,
  A-vaifin' de panners like efery dings.
De preeze droo de bine-trees is cooler und
  salt,
  Und der Shen'ral is merry venefer ve halt;
Loosty und merry he schmells at de preeze,
  Lustig und heiter[1] he looks droo de drees,
Lustig und heiter ash vell he may pe,
  For Sherman, at last, has march't down to
  de sea !

Dere 's a gry from de guard·—dere 's a clotter
  und dramp,

----

[1] Lighthearted and cheerful.

Ven dat fery same orterly rides droo de
camp,
Who report on de ford.   Dere ish druples and
awe
In de face of de youf' apout somedings he
saw ;
Und he shpeak me in Fraentsch, like he always do : ' Look !
Sagre pleu ! fentre-Tieu[1]—dere ish Breitmann—his spook ![2]
He ish goming dis vay !   *Nom de gare !*[3] can
it pe
Dat de spooks of de tead men coom down
to de sea !'

[1] *Sacre-bleu, ventre-Dieu :* Fr. Burlesque oaths.
[2] Ghost or fetch.
[3] *Nom de guerre :* Fr. ' Fighting name,' nickname, but
here used mistakenly for an oath.

Und ve looks, und ve sees, und ve tremples
    mit tread,
For risin' all schwart[1] on de efenin' red
Vas Johannes—der Breitmann—der war es,[2]
    bei Gott!
Coom ridin' to oos-vard, right shtraight to
    de shpot!
All mouse-schtill ve shtood, yet mit oop-
    shoompin' hearts,
For he look shoost so pig as de shiant of
    de Hartz;
Und I heard de Sout'-Deutschers say, 'Ave
    Morie![3]
Braise Gott all goot shpirids py land und
    py sea!'

[1] Black.   [2] 'Der war es :' *Ger.* 'There he was !'
[3] The 'Sud-Deutschers,' or inhabitants of Southern Germany, are mostly Catholics.

Boot Itzig of Frankfort he lift oop his nose,

  Und be-mark[1] dat de shpook hat peen
    changin' his clothes,

For he zeemed like an Generalissimus drest

  In a vlamin' new coat und magnificent
    vest.

Six bistols beschlagen mit silber[2] he vore,

  Und a cold-mounded swordt like a Kaisar[3]
    he bore,

Und ve dinks dat de ghosdt—or votever he
    pe—

  Moosht haf proken some panks[4] on his vay
    to de sea.

---

[1] Bemerken, to notice.

[2] Covered or inlaid with silver ; Damasceened.

[3] 'Like an emperor.'

[4] 'Broken some banks,' a perversion of the gamblers'
phrase to make it signify 'committed some robbery.'

'Id is he !' '*Und er lebt noch !*'—he lifs, ve all
  say :

Der Breitmann—Oldt Breitmann !—Hans
  Breitmann ! '*Herr Je !*'[1]

Und ve roosh to emprace him, und shtill more
  ve find

Dat verefer he'd peen, he'd left noding
  pehind.

In bofe of his poots dere vas porte-moneys
  crammed,

Mit creen-packs stoof-full all his haversack
  jammed,

In his bockets cold dollars vere shinglin' dein
  doons

Mit doo doozen votches und four dozer
  shpoons,

[1] ' 'Lord Jesus !'

Und doo silber tea-pods for makin' his dea,
  Der ghosdt haf pring mit him, *en route* to
  de sea.

Mit goot sweed-botatoes,[1] und doorkies, und
  rice,
  Ve makes him a sooper of efery-dings nice.
Und de bummers hoont roundt apout, *alle wie
  ein,*[2]
  Dill dey findt a plantaschion mit parrels of
  wein.
Den 'tvas 'here's to you, Breitmann! Alt
  Schwed—*bist zurück?*[3]
  Vot teufels you makes since dis fourteen
  nights veek?'

[1] Sweet potatoes are yams or plaintains.
[2] All like one man.
[3] 'Old chum, you've got back again?'

Und ve holds von shtupendous und derriple
 shpree
For choy dat der Breitmann has cot to de sea.

But in fain tid we ashk vhere der Breitmann
 hat peen,
 Vot he tid ; vot he bass droo—or vot he
  might seen ?
Vere he kits his vine horse, or who gafe him
 dem woons,
 Und how Brovidence plessed him mit tea-
  pods und shpoons ?
For to all of dem queeries he only reblies,
 ' If you dells me no quesdions, I ashks you
  no lies !'
So 'twas glear dat some derriple mysh'dry
 moost pe

Vere he kits all dat bloonder he prings to
de sea.

Dere ish bapers in Richmond dells derriple lies
How Sherman's grand armee haf raise deir
  sooplies :
For ve readt *in brindt* dat der Sheneral
  Grant
Say de Bummers[1] haf only shoost take vat
  dey vant.

[1] 'Bummer' in time had come to be derived anew from a
supposed verb to 'bum,' implying 'to *sit* about or lean upon
the barrels in a drinking-place.' Hence, 'bummers' were
properly such characters as become pillars of public-houses
— counter or bar props ;— never working, yet picking up
stray coppers from day to day ; without visible or legitimate
means of livelihood, yet always existing. So the scouts of
Sherman's army, who led the way without 'falling back' or
'sending in' for regular rations, but subsisting mysteriously
on the enemy, were pre-eminently 'Bummers.'

But 'tis vispered dat vile a refolfer'll go round
  Der BREITMANN vill nefer a-peggin' be
    found;
Or shtarvin' ash bris'ner—by doonder!—not
  he,
Vile der Teufel could help him to ged to de
  sea.

BREITMANN IN KANSAS.

VONCE oopon a dimes, good while afder
der Var vas ofer, der Herr Breitmann
vent oud Vest, drafellin' apout like efery-dings
—'*circuivit terram et perambulavit eam,*' ash
der Teufel said ven dey ask him : ' How vash
you and how you has peen ?'

Von efening she vas drafel niit some ladiesh
und shendlemans, und he shtaid *incognitus.*
Und dey sing'd songs, dill py-und-py one of
de ladiesh say : ' Ish any podies here ash
know de crate pallad of Hans Breitmann's

Barty?' Den Hans say : '*Ecce Gallus!* I
am dat rooster!'[1] Den der Hans dook a
trink und a let-bencil und a biece of baper,
and goes indo himself a little dimes[2] and den
coomes out again mit dis boem :

Hans Breitmann vent to Kansas;
   He drafel vast und var.
He rided shoost drei[3] dousand miles
   All in von rail-roat car.
He knowed foost-rate how far he goed —
   He gounted all de vile,
Dere vash shoost one pottle of champagne,
   Dat bopped at efery mile.

---

[1] ' Rooster.' *American* for cock-a-doodle-doo, or the sultan
of the barn fowl.
[2] Free translation of *se retirer*.   [3] Three.

Hans Breitmann vent to Kansas ;

I tell you vot, my poy,

You bet dey hat a pully[1] dimes

In crossin' Illinoy.[2]

Dey speaked deir speaks to all de volk

A-shtandin' in de car ;

Den ashk dem in do dake a trink,

Und corned em *ganz und gar.*[3]

Hans Breitmann vent to Kansas ;

[1] Bully.   A slang term for 'capital,' 'excellent ;' not only popular throughout the North American continent, but in Paris in 1868–9 as 'du bœuf.'

[2] The State of Illinois, as generally pronounced.   This State is mentioned here on account of the Illinois Central Railroad, over which Breitmann is made to travel on his way to Kansas.

[3] 'Made them thoroughly drunk ;' from 'to corn,' to pickle with *corn* (maize) whisky.

By shings![1] dey did it prown.
When he got into Leafenvort,[2]
He found himselv in town.
Dey dined him at de Blanter's House,
 Moor goot as man could dink;
Mit efery dings on eart' to eat,
 Und dwice as mooch to trink.

Hans Breitmann vent to Kansas;
He vent it on de loud.[3]
At Ellsvort', in de prairie land,
He foundt a pully crowd.

---

[1] 'By Jing,' for Jingo.
[2] Leavenworth.
[3] To 'travel on the loud,' to journey in a showy, flash
manner.   A cockneyism recently imported by the New
Yorkers in return for certain Americanisms which have
been adopted here.

He looked for bleedin' Kansas,[1]
 But dat's 'blayed out,' dey say;
De vhiskey-keg's de only dings
 Dat's bleedin' dere to-day.

Hans Breitmann vent to Kansas,
 To see vot he could hear.
He foundt some Deutschers dat exisdt
 Py makin' lager-peer.
Says he : ' *Wie gehts, du Alt Gesell?*'[2]
 But nodings could be heard;
Dey'd growed so fat in Kansas
 Dat dey couldn't speak a vord.

[1] Kansas was called 'bleeding' because of supposed tyranny from the Southerners, who occupied the country along with slave-detesting Yankees.
[2] 'How are you, my old buck?'

Hans Breitmann vent to Kansas;
  Py shings! I dell you vot,
Von day he met a crisly bear
  Dat rooshed him down, *bei Gott!*
Boot der Breitmann took und bind der bear,
  Und bleased him fery much—
For efery vordt der crisly growled
  Vas goot Bavarian Dutch!

Hans Breitmann vent to Kansas;
  By doonder dat is so!
He ridet oot upon de blains
  To shase de boofalo.
He fired his rifle at de bools,
  Und gallop droo de shmoke,
Und shoomp de canyons[1] shoost as if
  Der teufel vas a choke!

---

[1] 'Canyon:' English spelling of the pronunciation of American-Spanish, *cañon*, a ravine.

It's hey de trail to Santa Fé;
  It's ho! agross de blain;
It's lope[1] along de Denver Road,
  Until ve toorn again,
Und de railroad drafel after us
  Apout as quick as ve;
Dis Kansas ish de vastest land
  Ash efer I did see.

Hans Breitmann vent to Kansas;
  He haf a pully[2] dime;
Bot 'tvas in old Missouri
  Dat dey rooshed him up[3] sublime.

---

[1] 'To lope:' ancient preterit of 'to leap;' but Western hunters think it is from the peculiar steady swinging trot of a wolf (Canadian French 'lope' for 'loup') in the chase.

[2] 'Bully:' fine, jolly.

[3] '*To rush it,* to do a thing with spirit.'—BARTLETT.

Dey took him to der Bilot Knob,
Und all der knobs around ;
Dey shpreed him und dey tea'd him
Dill dey roon him to de ground.

Hans Breitmann vent to Kansas;
Droo all dis earthly land,
A-vorkin' out life's mission here
Soobyectifly und grand.
Some beoblesh runs de beautiful,
Some vorks philosophie ;
Der Breitmann solf de infinide
Ash von eternal shpree !

SHTORY

APOUT

SCHNITZERL'S PHILOSOPEDE.

HERR SCHNITZERL make a philo-
sopede,
Von of der newest kindt;
It vent mitout a vheel in vront,
Und hadn't none pehind.
Von vheel vas in de mittel, dough,
Und it vent as sure ash ecks,
Vor he shtraddled on de axel dree
Mit der vheel petween his lecks.

Und ven he vant to shtart id off
    He paddlet mit his veet,
Und soon he cot to go so vast
    Dat avery dings he peat.
He run her out on Broader shtreet,
    He shkeeted like de vind,
Hei! how he bassed de vancy traps,
    Und lef dem all pehind!

De vellers mit de trotting nags
    Pooled oop to see him bass:
De Deutschers all erstaunished saidt:
    '*Potztausend! Was ist das?*'
Boot vaster shtill der Schnitzerl flewed
    On — mit a gashtly smile;
He tidn't tooch de dirt, py shings!
    Not vonce in half a mile.

Oh, vot ish all dis eartly pliss?
　Oh, vot ish man's soocksess?
Oh, vot ish various kinds of dings?
　Und vot ish habbiness?
Ve find a pank note in de shtreedt,
　Next dings der pank ish preak;
Ve falls, und knocks our outsides in,
　Ven ve a ten shtrike make.[1]

So vas it mit der Schnitzerlein
　On his philosopede;
His feet both shlipped outsideward shoost.
　Ven at his extra shpede.
He felled oopon der vheel of coorse;

---

[1] Ten strike, the master stroke at the bowling game of ten pins,—a variation of our English skittles. Here instanced as an enviable success in life—a decided hit.

De vheel like blitzen[1] flew ;
Und Schnitzerl he vos schnitz[2] in vact,
Vor id slished hid him guide in two.

Und as for his philosopede,
Id cot so shkared, men say,
It pounded onward till it vent
Ganz teufelwards[3] afay,
Boot vhere ish now der Schnitzerl's soul ?
Vhere dos his shbirit pide ?
In Himmel[4] troo de endless plue,
It takes a medeor ride.

[1] ' Blitz :' *Ger*. Lightning.
[2] ' Schnitz :' *Ger*. A slice, a cut.
[3] Entirely, or completely, in the direction of the Devil.
[4] ' Himmel :' *Ger*. Heaven,

BALLAD OF THE MERMAID.

BY HANS BREITMANN.

D ER noble Ritter[1] Hugo
　　Von Schwillensaufenstein,
Rode out mit shpeer und helmet,
　　Und he coom to de panks of de Rhine.

Und oop dere rose a meer-maid,
　　Vot hadn't got nodings on,
Und she say, ' Oh, Ritter Hugo,
　　Vhere you goes mit yourself alone ?'

[1] Knight, Sir.

Und he says, ' I rides in de creenwood,
  Mit helmet und mit shpeer,
Till I gooms into ein Gasthaus,[1]
  Und dere I trinks some peer.'

Und den outsphoke de maiden
  Vot hadn't got nodings on :
' I ton't dink mooch of beoplesh
  Dat goes mit demselfs alone.

' You 'd petter coom down in de wasser,
  Vhere dere 's heaps of dings to see,
Und haf a shplendid tinner
  Und drafel along mit me.

---

[1] Tavern, or wine-shop.

'Dere you sees de fisch a-schwimmin',
  Und you catches dem efery one :'—
So sang dis wasser maiden
  Vot hadn't got nodings on.

'Dere ish drunks all full mit money
  In ships dat vent down of old ;
Und you helpsh yourself, by doonder!
  To shimmerin' [1] crowns of gold.

'Shoost look at dese shpoons und vatches!
  Shoost see dese diamant rings !
Goom down and vill your bockets,
  Und I'll giss you like efery dings.

---

[1] 'Schimmern:' *Ger.* To glitter, to sparkle, to glimmer.

'Vot you vantsh mit your schnaps[1] und lager?
Coom down into der Rhine!
Der ish pottles der Kaiser Charlemagne
Vonce filled mit gold-red wine!'

Dat fetched him[2]—he shtood all shpell-pound!
She pooled his coat-tails down,
She drawed him oonder der wasser,
De maiden mit nodings on.

---

[1] 'Schnapps:' *Ger.* Drams, drinks.
[2] 'Brought him to a determination,' emphatically.

DIE SCHŒNE WITTWE.

(DE POOTY VIDDER.)

I. VOT DE YANKEE CHAP SUNG.

D AT pooty liddle vidder
   Vot ve doshn't vish to name,
Ish still leben[1] on dat liddle shtreet,
   A-doin' shoost de same.
De glerks aroundt de gorners
   Somedimes goes round to zee
How die tarlin' liddle vitchy ees,
   Und ask 'er how she pe.
Dey lufs her ver' goot liqoor,
   Dey lufs her liddle shtore;

[1] 'Leben,' living.

Dey lufs her little paby,
But dey lufs die vidder more.
To dalk mit dat shveet vidder,
Ven she hands das lager round,
Vill make der shap dat does id
Pe happy, ve'll be pound.
Dat ish, if we can vell pelieve
De glerks vat drinks das pier,
Who goes in dere for noding elshe,
Put simply vor to zee her.

II. HOW DER BREITMANN CUT HIM OUT.

OH, yes, I know die wittwe,
Mit eyes so prite und proun!

She's de allerschœnste wittwe[1]
  Vot lif in dis here down.
In her plack silk gown—mine grashious !—
  All puttoned to de neck —
Und a pooty liddle collar,
  Mitout a shpot or spheck.
Ho ! clear de drack,[2] you oder *fraus*—
  You gan't pekin to shine
Vhen de lufly vidder cooms along —
  Dis vidder ash ish mine !
Ho ! clear de drack, you Yankee shaps,
  You Englishers und sooch.
You can't pekin to coot me out,
  Mitout you dalks in Dootch.

---

[1] Most-beautiful widow.
[2] 'Clear the track,' railway slang ; in English 'clear the line.'

Ich hab die schœne wittwe
  Schon lange nit gesehn,
Ich sah sie gestern Abend
  Wohl bei dem Counter stehn.
Die Wangen rein wie Milch and Blut,
  Die Augen hell und klar.
Ich hab sie sechsmal auch geküsst—
  Potztausend ! das ist wahr.[1]

[1] These eight lines may be roughly translated as follows :—

  I had not seen the pretty widow
    For a long time ;
  But last evening I saw her,
    Standing gracefully behind the counter.
  Her cheeks were as pure and ruddy
    As milk and blood could make them.
  Her eyes were beautifully bright and clear.
  Did I give her as many as *six* kisses ?
    Upon my word, I believe I did !

F

HANS BREITMANN'S CHRISTMAS.

'Hæc est illa bona dies
Et vocata læta quies
Vina sitientibus.

'Nullus metus, nec labores,
Nulla cura, nec dolores,
Sint in hoc symposio.'
*[De Generibus Ebriosorum, Francoforti
ad Mænum, A.D.* 1565.

I D vas on Weihnachtsabend—vot Ghrist-
mas Efe dey.call—
Der Breitmann mit his Breitmen tid rent¹ de
Musik Hall;

¹ 'Rent,' for to lease, to hire—a common form of
expression in America.

Ash de Breitmen und die vomen who vere
    in de Liederkranz[1]
Vouldt blend deir souls in harmonie to have
    a bleasin' tantz.

Dey reefed[2] de Hall 'mid pushes so nople to
    pe seen,
Aroundt Beethoven's buster dey on-did[3] a
    garlandt creen;
De laties vork like tyfels doo tays to scroob
    de vloor,

[1] The 'Liederkranz' is a German choral union. The
principal American section holds its meetings in New York,
and the annual ball of this glee society is the most
recherché of all the public festivities of the Germans in
that great city.

[2] They *wreathed* the hall.

[3] 'On-did,' *i.e.* the *German*, anthun, to put on; used with
an oblique reference to the Americanism 'fix:'—'they fixed a
garland on the bust.'

Und hanged a crate serenity[1] mit *WILL-COMM !*[2] oop de toor !

Und vhile dere vas a Schwein-blatt[3] whose redakteur[4] tid say ;
Dat Breitmann he vas *liederlich;*[5] ve antworded[6] dis-away,
Ve maked anoder serenity mid ledders plue und red :

[1] A transparency, from 'serene' being taken in its meaning of clear.

[2] *Ger.* 'Willkommen.' Welcome.

[3] Term of contempt for a newspaper : the dirty paper, or the 'Hog's Journal.'

[4] 'Redacteur,' editor. A French word lately adopted by the Germans.

[5] Loose or reckless. Precisely the word for what are called 'scaliwags' in the United States.

[6] 'Antworded,' ' Wir antworteten :' *Ger.* We answered.

'*OUR LEADER LICK DE REPELS!*
N.G.' (enof gesaid.)[1]

Und anoder serene dransbarency ve make de
    veller baint,
Boot de vay he potch und vertyfeled[2] id, vas
    enof to shvear a saint,
For ve vanted *LA GERMANIA;* boot der
    ardist, mit a bloonder,
Vent und vlorished LAGER agross id—und
    denn poot *MANIA* oonder!

Und as Ghristmas Efe vas gekommen,[3] de
    beoples weren im Hall;

---

[1] A variation of the English and American street humour.
'N. C.'—*nuf ced*.
[2] Bedevilled.
[3] 'Gekommen:' *Ger*. Was come, had arrived.

I shvears you, **id** vas Gott-full[1]—dat shplen-
dit, pe-glory'd ball ;
Ve hat foon *wie der Teufel in Frankreich*[2]—
ve coot oop like der tyfel in France,[2]
Und valk pair-wise in, vhile de musik blayed
loudt de Fackel-Tanz.[3]

Boot vhen de valtz shtrike oopwart ve most
went out of fits,

[1] Divine.

[2] The proverb—A great frolic, like the devil in France;
equivalent to our ' As lively as the devil among the tailors.'

[3] Flambeaux or torch dance. In Germany, after a procession, the torch-bearers meet in an open space—generally
the market-place—and form a circle of two or three deep,
according to the number taking part in the affair. The inner
circle pitch their torch-ends into the middle of the ring,
which is immediately followed by the outer circles throwing
their torch-ends in the same direction, over the heads of the
persons before them. Around the bonfire thus formed the
students, or those engaged, hold their *Fackel-Tanz*.

Ash der Breitmann led off on a dwister mit
de luffly Helmina[1] Schmitz.
He valtz shoost like he vas shtandin shtill,
mit a peaudiful solemn shmile,
Und 'Mina say he nefer shtop *poussiren*[2] alla
weil.

'*Es tœnt, es rauschet Saitenklang*—I hear de
musik call
Den kerzenhellen Saal entlang—all droo de
gleamin' Hall.
O mœcht ich schweben stolz und froh—O
mighdt I efer pe

---

[1] Wilhelmina,—generally shortened to *Helmina* or *Mina*.
[2] To pay attention to, to court; but there is also an
allusion to the French dancing term '*pousser.*'

Mit dir durchs ganze Leben so!—mine Lebenlang[1] by dee !'

Und vaster blay de musik[2] de *Wellen und
Wogen*[3] von Strauss ;
Und soom drop indo[4] de tantzen,[5] und
soom of dem drop *aus ;*[6]
Und soon like a shtorm in de Meere[7] I veel
de reelin' vloor,

[1] 'Mein Lebenlang.' My lifetime long, all my life.
[2] 'The music,' for the band, the collective body of mu-
sicians. Heard in London theatres, from the gallery, ' Now,
then, play up, music !'
[3] A well-known waltz by this popular composer: ' The
Waves and the Billows.'
[4] 'Drop into,' a variation of the more common dancing
phrase ' fall into.'
[5] Dance.
[6] Out, on the floor, down.
An ocean storm.

So de shpinners shtop mit de shpinsters, for
    dey couldn't shpin no more.

Now weren ve all frolic, *und lauter guter
    ding,* [1]
Und dirsty ash a broosh-pinder [2]—ven ve
    hear some glasses ring;
Foorst mildt und sonft [3] in de distants—like
    de song of a nightingall,
Den a ringin' und rottlin' und clotterin'—
    ash de Glück of Edenhall! [4]

---

[1] 'And all in the best of humour.'

[2] 'Brush-binder:' burlesque German for brush-maker—
one who, from the dusty nature of his business, is popularly
believed to be as perpetually thirsty as the hatter is believed
to be mad.   The correct German is 'Bürstenbinder.'

[3] '*Mild und sanft,*' mild and gentle.

[4] 'The Luck of Edenhall,' by Uhland, translated by
Longfellow.   The Musgrave family, in Cumberland, possess
the cup of the legend.

Hei ! how ve roosh on de liquor !—hei ! how
de kellners[1] coom :

Hei ! how ve busted de bier-kegs und poon-
ished de *Punsch à la Rhum.*[2]

Like lonely wafes at mitternight oopon some
shiant shore ;

Like an awful shtorm in de Wælder[3]—vas
de dirsty Deutschers' roar !

I pyed some carts for a dime[4] abiece—I
pyed shoost fifdy-dwo,

[1] Waiters.

[2] 'Ponche à la rhum,' (or, more correctly speaking,
'Punch au rhum') rum-punch, figures in many Paris bills
of fare for late suppers.

[3] In the forests or woods.

[4] 'Dime,' ten cents United States' currency. From the
French *dixme,* or *dîme,* tenth. A Dime is the tenth of a
dollar. The term arose in New Orleans and those Southern
towns which were once within the old French colony.

Dey vere goot for[1] bier, or schnapps, or
    wein; by doonder, how dey flew!
I ring de deck[2] on de vaiters for liquor hot
    und cool,
Und efery dime I blays a cart, py shings, I
    rake de pool![3]

---

[1] · Good for,' Americanism, 'redeemable in.' During
the opening year of the great civil war, when specie was
withdrawn, and the Government had not met the demand by
increased issue of paper-money or small coin, many trade
tokens were issued. The car-conductors (tramway-cads)
were the most particular about taking dubious pseudo-
change, and, on one of them being offered a ticket of another
company, he said, 'That won't pass here — it's the Eighth
Avenue: only good for Macomb's Dam!' (a place on the
Harlem River, upper end of New York City). 'Only good
for Macomb's *Dam?*' repeated the owner, disconsolately.
'Well, friend, I *coin*-cide! I believe *that's* all it is *good for!'*

[2] *Deck* of cards is usually applied to such a portion of a
complete pack as may be required for a particular game.

[3] 'Rake de pool,' from the croupier's *rake* at roulette.

Und ash ve trinked so comforble, like boogs
in any roog,[1]
De trompets blowed *tan da ra dei*, und dere
come in a *Maskenzug*,[2]
A peaudiful brocession, soul-raisin' und soo-
plime,
De marmorbilds[3] of de heroes of de early
Sharman dime.

Dere vent der gros Arminius,[4] mit his frau
Thusnelda, doo,

---

[1] 'Bugs in a rug,' Irish expression for the height of snug-
ness.
[2] A train or procession of persons masquerading.
[3] 'Marmorbild,' a statue or bust in marble.
[4] Hermann, the ancient German leader who defeated the
Roman army under Varus.

De vellers ash lam[1] de Romans dill dey roon
mit noses plue,

Den vollowed Quinctilius Varus who carry a
Roman yoke,

Und ᵢarm in arm mit Gambrinus[2] coom der
Allemane Chroc.[3]

---

[1] 'Lam:' *Old E.* to beat.   Often spoken as 'lambaste'
in the United States.

[2] Gambrinus, the tun-bellied King of Beer—and of
Bavaria—is a favourite toast in German song.   His rotund
figure gives a shape to many a German beer-mug.

[3] 'Allemane Chroc:' *Ger.* Alemannischer Krug, a German jug or tankard, of the shape described in the pre-
ceding note.   The king embodied in the jug—Krug (or
'Chroc') and Gambrinus accompanying each other—Breitmann thought might be well described by the words 'arm-
in-arm.'   Chroc.—*Ger.* Krug (*Patois*, Krog); *Old Engl.*
Crock; *Anglo-Sax.* Crocca. (See *Adelung Wörterbuch.*)

[The editor of another edition of the present volume—a
German by birth—says: '*Chroc.*—An Alemannic hero
unknown to history' (!)]

Der alte Friedrich Rothbart,[1] und Kaiser
Karl der Crate,[2]
Mit Roland und Uliverus,[3] vent shveepin' on
in shtate ;
Und Conradin,[4] whose sad-full deat' shtill
makes our heartsen pleed,
Und all ov dem oldt vellers aus dem Nibelun-
gen Lied.[5]

Und as dey mofed on, der Breitmann maked
a tyfeled shplendid witz[6]

[1] Barbarossa.
[2] Charlemagne.
[3] Roland and Oliver.
[4] Prince Konradin (Conrad), who was beheaded at Naples,
in 1268.
[5] 'The Lay of the Nibelungen.'
[6] 'Tyfeled shplendid witz.' In plain English, 'A deuced
good pun !' As some indication of the extent to which

In anti-word[1] to dis quesdion from de lofely
'Mina Schmitz :—
'Vhy ish id dey always makes in shtone dem
vellers so andiquatet ?'
'Vhy? Dey set in de laps of Ages dill dey
got lapi*dated !*'

Und shoost ash de last of dis hisdory hat
fanished droo de toor,

German speech has affected the vernacular in America, we
may state that this German word, *witz*, has been adopted by
the vast numbers of 'negro minstrels' in the United States,
and also by their representatives in this country. Those
casual (make-believe impromptu) jokes and puns indulged in
by theatricals are styled 'gags;' amongst minstrels they are
known as '*wheezes.*' Hence the sally of the 'end man,'
at Christy's: 'Why is an asthmatic man the funniest of all
the doctor's patients? Because he is full of *wheezes !*'

[1] Antwort: *Ger.* Answer.

Ve heardt a ge-screech,[1] und Pelz Nickel[2]
coom howlin' on de vloor ;
Den de laties yell like der tyfel, und vly like
gulls mit vings,

[1] Ge-screech. A corruption, or twisting, of the *Ger.* Ge-schrei : shriek, scream.

[2] Pelz Nickel is the fur-coated St. Nicholas, whom we see as a toy figure, hooded, and with his coat lined with fur, in our shop-windows—especially at Mr. Rimmel's, the per-fumer—about Christmas time. He usually bears a tree —the Christmas tree of children—and is believed in German nurseries to pass over the house-tops on the night of the 5th of December, and to drop down the chimney nice presents for good children and rods to whip bad ones. It is usual to place a stocking in the fireplace to receive Pelz Nickel's gifts, and mamma and papa generally avail themselves of the occasion to show their pleasure or displeasure at the conduct of little master or miss during the past year. The toy figure imported here from Germany has been re-named by our children ' Old Father Christmas.' In America he is better known as ' Santa Claus (Nic*klaus*), and the time of his appearance has been altered to Christmas Eve.

G

Und der Pelz Nickel lick[1] em mit svitches,[2]
und ve laughet like efery dings.

I nefer hafe sooch laughen before dat I vas
ge-born ;
Und Pelz Nickel, vhen 'tvas ober, he blow on
a yæger horn,[3]
Und denounce[4] do all de beople gesembled in
de hall :--
'Dat a Ghristmas dree vas vaiten', mit presents for oos all !'

---

[1] Lick, respectable old English for 'to beat,' but now a vulgar expression, quite as common in the United States as here.

[2] In America the word 'rod' or 'birch' is seldom used. Children are always beaten with 'switches.'

[3] A huntsman's horn.

[4] A Malapropism which needs no explanation.

So ve vollowed him into de zimmer¹ so quick
ash dese vords he said,
To kit dem peaudiful bresents, all gratis und
on de dead ;²

Zimmer: *Ger.* Room.

² 'On the dead.' A most curious Americanism, which Mr. Trübner has found himself entirely unable to explain. It is, in reality, a contraction of another Transatlantic expression: 'DEAD HEAD,' a person who rides, drinks, or eats without paying anything for the same, or who has a free pass to the theatre or the railway. The gentlemen of the press, from their rarely paying for their amusements, their carriage, or their feed, by reason of their influence and official positions, are 'dead heads.' Bartlett gives this extract:—

'The principal avenue of our city,' writes a learned friend in Detroit, 'has a toll-gate just by the Elmwood Cemetery road. As the cemetery had been laid out some time previous to the construction of the plank-road, it was made one of the conditions of the company's charter that all funeral processions should go back and forth free. One day as Dr. Price, a celebrated physician, stopped to pay his toll, he remarked to the gate-keeper:—" Considering the benevolent character of our profession, I think you ought to let us pass free of charge."

' "No, no, doctor," the keeper readily replied—' 'we couldn't afford that; you send too many DEAD HEADS through here as it is !"

'The doctor paid his toll, and never asked favours after that.'

Washington Evening Star, Oct. 1857.

Hence to get anything '*on the dead*' is to obtain it free of charge.

Und in facdt a shplendid Weihnachtsbaum[1]
mit lighds ve druly vound,
Und liddel kifts dat ge-kostet a benny abiece
all roundt !

Dere vas Rika Stange die Dessauerinn[2]—a
maedchen[3] shtraigdt und tall,
She cot a bicture of Cubid—boot she tidnt
see it ad all[4]

[1] Weihnachtsbaum : *Ger.*   A Christmas tree.
[2] The girl from Dessau.
[3] Mädchen : *Ger.*   Maiden.
[4] 'Did not *see* it,' viz. would not allow it to be observed.
That is, she *would not* see the pleasantry intended, she
would not commit herself.   The word *see* is often used here
in this way : thus, if one man is trying to persuade another
against his will, the other exclaims, 'I don't *see* it !' *i.e.* 'I
don't *see it in that light*—I don't understand the matter as
you explain it.'

Dill der Breitmann say, mit his shplendid
    shtyle dat all de laties dake :—
'Dat pend of de bow ish de Crecian pend[1]
    dat you so ofden make !'

Anoder scharmante laity, Maria Top, did cot,
A-schwingin' mit a ribbon, a liddle benny
    pot ;
Boot Breitmann haff id de roughest of any
    oder mans,

---

[1] 'The Grecian bend.' A recent Paris fashion, at once
adopted in America. It is the curve made at the back of the
body when a female carries herself as if walking in a per-
petual curtesy. By ornamenting a sash with a large bow on
the apex of this bend, or by a puff of the dress over-skirt, it
is made still more exquisitely Hottentot Venus-like. It may
just be remarked that as the Irish are known as 'the Greeks'
in America, to 'go on the Grecian bender is to get drunk
on Irish whisky.

For he kit a yellow gratle mit a liddle vooden
Hans.[1]

Den next Beethoven's Sinfonie, die orkester
tid blay ;
Adagio—allegro—andante cantabile.
Ve sat in shtill commotion so dat a bin
mighdt drops,
Und de deers roon town der Breitmann's
sheeks, mitwhiles he vas trinkin'
schnapps.[2]

Next dings ve had de *Weinnachtstraum*[3] ge-
sung by de Liederkranz ;[4]

[1] Hans, the commonest of all German Christian names :
equivalent to our John, Johnny.

[2] Schnapps: *Ger.*   A dram, a drink of strong liquor.

[3] A pun.   'Weinnachtstraum,' wine night's dream—for
Weihnachtstraum, Christmas night's dream.

[4] The glee society.

Denn I trinked dwelf schoppens[1] of glee-
wine[2] to sed me oop for a tantz ;
Dis dimes I tanz wie der Tyfel[3]—we shriek[4]
de volk on de vloor ;
Und boost right indo de sooper room—for ve
tanzt a hole troo de door !

Denn 'twas rowdy tow[5] und hop-sasa,[6] ve
hollered, Mann und Weib ;[7]

[1] Schoppen, *Ger.* chopin. A measure, a pint.
[2] Glühwein : *Ger.* Mulled or spiced wine.
[3] Teufel : *Ger.* The devil. The favourite word in the German speech of the lower orders. For purposes of comparison it is being continually employed—everything being as fast or slow, good or bad, as 'der Teufel.' It is, however, in almost as much requisition for swearing purposes.
[4] Schrecken : *Ger.* To frighten, to alarm.
[5] 'Row-de-dow,' imitation of a drum-beat, from the popular American song, 'Whack-row-de-dow ! I'm a Gentleman of the Army !'
[6] Hopsa ! Interjection of excitement, without any particular meaning; hey-day !
[7] 'Man and wife ;' but this is scarcely the author's mean-

'Rip, Sam, und sed her oop acain!¹—ve 'er

all of de Shackdaw tribe !'

Vhen Pelz Nickel plow his trump vonce more,

und peg oos to shtop our din,

Und troo de oben toor dere coomed nine

den-pins marchin' in.²

ing. 'Every mother's son of us' would suit the occasion
better, but those words would not fit the rhyme.

¹ The English reader will be puzzled not a little at this
outburst.   It is the chorus of the favourite song of the
American bowling-alleys —

    'Rip, Sam, set her up again, set her up again, set her up again!
    Rip, Sam, set her up again! we are all of the Choctaw tribe!'

'Let her rip, Sam,' *i.c.* 'roll the ball down;' 'set her up
again,' *i.e.* 'stick up the pin or pins again.'   All the men
who perform the office of 'sticking-up' rejoice in the name
of 'Sam.'   It is not generally known that our recently
famous music-hall song of 'Jolly Dogs' was taken from the
American 'Rip, Sam.'

² Ten-pins.   A game similar to our Nine-pins

Nine vellers tressed like den-pins—dey goed
    to de end' der hall,
Und dwo Hans Wurst,[1] shack-puddin' glowns
    —dey rolled at 'em mit a pall.
De palls vas baintet peaudiful; dey was vif-
    deen feet aroundt;
Und de rule ov de came : 'whoefer cot hidt,
    moost doomple on de croundt.'

Somedimes dey hit de den-pins—somedimes
    de oder volk—
Und pooty soon de gompany vas all laid out
    in shoke ;

[1] Literally Jack-puddings—merry-Andrews, buffoons, the clowns with bladders tied to the ends of sticks, or those who could make and swallow imaginary sausages of an extravagant length.

Boot I dells you vot, it maked oos laugh dill
　　ve py-nearly shplits,
Vhen der Breitmann, he roll ofer, und drip
　　oop de 'Mina Schmitz.

Dis lets itself in Sharman pe foost-rade word-
　　blayed on,[1]
Und 'mongst oos be-giftet vellers you pet dat
　　id vas tone !
How der Breitmann mighdt drafel ash bride-
　　mann on de roadt dat ish *breit* und
　　krumm :[2]
Here de drumpets soundt, und pair-wise ve
　　goed for[3] de sooper-room.

[1] 'Jeu de mot,' pun ; *Ger.* Wortspiel
[2] The *broad* and *crooked* way.
[3] 'To go for.'　To seize, to rush at, an Americanism.

Ve goed for ge-roasted Welsh-hens,[1] ve goed
for gespickter hare,[2]
Ve goed for kartoffel[3] salade mit butter brod
— Kaviar :[4]
Ve roosh at de lordtly sauer-kraut[5] und de
wurst[6] vitch lofely shine,

---

[1] Welsche Hahn. The Italian [all things foreign to Germany were attributed to Italy] turkey-cock. The author may intend a pun here at Welsh-*rabbit* (rare-bit) in connection with the *hare* following.

[2] Roast hare larded or punctured with thin strips of bacon. Spicken: *Ger.* To interlard.

[3] Kartoffel: *Ger.* Potato.

[4] Caviar, the roe of the sturgeon pickled. A favourite delicacy, imported from Russia.

[5] Sauerkraut, the German national dish—cabbage pickled in brine, not vinegar.

[6] Wurst: *Ger.* Sausage,—here one of the shining kind. washed with the glare of an egg.

Und oh, mein Gott in Kimmel![1] *how* we goed
for de Mosel-wein![2]

Und troonker more, und troonker yet, und
troonker shtill cot ve,
In rosy lighdt shtill driven on agross a fairy
sea ;
Denn madder, vilder, frantic-er, I proked a
salat-dish !
Und shoost like roarin' elefants ve tanzt
aroundt de tish.[3]

[1] A pun upon 'Oh, mein Gott in Himmel!' (in heaven),
the tipsy songster confusing it with ' Kümmel,' familiar for
' Kümmel-wasser,' brandy flavoured with carraway seeds.
[2] 'Sparkling Moselle.'
[3] Tisch : *Ger.*   Table.

I'fe shvimmed in heafenly troonks pefore—
boot nefer von like dis,
De morgen-het-ache[1] only seemt a bortion of
de pliss.
De vhile in trilling peauty roundt like heafenly
vind-harps rang
A goosh of goldnen melodie—de Rhinewein-
bechers' Klang.[2]

De meltin' minnesingers'[3] song—a droonk of
honey'd rhyme—

[1] The morning head-ache— the 'hot coppers,' which seek relief in soda-and-brandy.

[2] The clash of the beakers brimming with good Rhine wine. Probably allusion is made to the popular song 'Rheinweinlied, words by M. Claudius, music by J. Andre (1771), usually sung at all German festivals when the company begin to get merry, and the Rhine wine is passing around the board.

[3] Minnesinger, a singer of love melodies in former times.

De b'wildrin-dipsy Bardic shants of Teuto-
   burgic dime ;
Back to de Runic dim Valhall[1] und Balder's
   foamin' mead :——
——Here ents in heller glorie schein des
   Breitmann's Weihnachtslied ![2]

[1] ' Valhall '—Walhalla, the banqueting-hall of the heroes
of Northern mythology.   ' Balder,' the son of Odin and
Friga, served out the foaming mead.
[2] ' Here ends, in the brightest blaze of glory, the song of
Breitmann's Christmas.'

DER FREISCHÜTZ.[1]

AIR—'*Der Pabst lebt*,' *&c.*[2]

WIE gehts,[3] my frendts—if you'll allow—
I sings you right afay shoost now
Some dretful shdories vitch dey calls
DER FREYSCHUTZ; or, de Magic Balls.

Wohl[4] in Bohemian landt it cooms,
Vhere folks trink prandy mate of plums;

[1] 'Der Freischütz,' the free archer of the olden time; in this case, the rifle-volunteer, of whom Weber's opera, named after him, immortalises the type.

[2] 'The Pope he leads a merry life,' rendered by Lever.

[3] How goes it, how are you, my friends?—equivalent to our 'How d'ye do?'

[4] Well.

Dere lifed ein Yaeger[1]—Maxerl[2] Schmit —
Who shot mit goons und nefer hit.

Und dere vas von oldt Yaeger, who
Says, 'Maxerl, dis vill nefer do ;
If you shouldt miss on trial-day,
Dere'll pe der tyfel denn to pay.

'If you do miss, you shtupid coose,
Dere'll pe de donnerwetter[3] loose ;

---

[1] Yaeger: *Ger.* Jäger, huntsman, sportsman.

[2] It may be as well to mention that the hero of this ballad is variously called *Max, Maxerl, Maximilian*—the two former being abbreviations of the latter. In Southern Germany 'Max*erl*' is the favourite form, the termination *erl* corresponding to our *ny* or *my* in such familiar renderings as John*ny*, Tom*my*.

[3] Donnerwetter. Thunder-weather, a tempest; the **ex**-pression is here used as a mild oath.

For you shan't haff mine taughter's hand,
Nor pe de Hertzhog's[1] yaegersmann.'[2]

Id coom'd pefore de tay vas set,
Dat all de chaps togeder met;
Und Maxerl fired his goon und missed,
Und all de gals cot roundt und hissed.

Dey laughed pefore und hissed pehind;
Boot von chap—Kaspar—saidt, 'Ton't mind;
I dells you vot—you stuns 'em alls
If yoost you shoodt mit magic balls.'

'De magic balls!—oh, vot is dat?'
'I got dem in my hoonting hat;

---

[1] Herzog: *Ger.*   A duke.
[2] Jägersmann: *Ger.*   Hunter, gamekeeper.

Dey're plack as kohl und shoodt so drue :
Oh, dem's de sort of palls for you !

'You see dat eagle vlyin' high,
Ein hoondred miles oop in de sky;
Shoot at dat eagle mit your bix,[1]
You kills him tead ash doonderblix !'[2]

'I ton't pelieve de dings you say.'
'You fool,' says Kass, 'denn plaze afay !'

---

[1] Bix, Büchse: *Ger.* Rifle. 'Bess,' 'Brown Bess,' the name given to the old regulation musket, is derived from the Dutch form of the word, and came from the Low Countries with William of Orange. When 'Hans *Busk* on the Rifle' was announced, a German publisher thought the name an assumed one for the sake of a pun.

[2] Doonderblix : *Ger.* Donner und Blitz : thunder and lightning.

He plazed afay, vhen, sure as plood,
Down coom'd de eagle in de mud.

' O was ist das ?' said Maxerl Schmit.[1]
' Vy ! dat's de eagle fot you hit.
You kills him vhen you plaze afay;
Boot dat's a ding you nix verstay.[2]

' Und you moost go to make dem balls
To de Wolf's Glen vhen mitnight falls.

[1] Oh, what is that ?

[2] Nichts, not; verstehen, to understand, to comprehend. ' Nix verstay,' is the popular or vulgar rendering of the correct phrase, as placed in the mouth of a newly-arrived German. ' Nongtongpaw' was formerly attributed to a Frenchman fresh from France, in the same way.

Dow know 'st de shpot—alone und late '—
' Oh, ya¹—I knows him *ganz*² foost-rate !'

' Boot denn I does not likes to go
Among dem dings.'   Says Kass, ' Ach, 'sho !³
I 'll help you fix dem tyfel chaps,
Like a goot feller—dake some schnapps !'

(' Hilf, Zamiel ! hilf !')⁴—' Here, trink some
   more !'
Der Kass vent shtompin' roundt de vloor,

¹ Ya: *Ger*.   Ja, yes.   To the reader unacquainted with German—and few in this country know the language when compared with the many Americans who speak it—we would remark that *j* in German always takes the sound of *y*, as jäger—yager; Johan—Yohan.

² Ganz: *Ger*.   Quite, entirely.

³ 'Ach, 'sho !' The parallel English exclamations, Ah! so! indeed! give the author's meaning.

⁴ ' Help, Zamiel ! [the demon] help!'   ' Come to my aid.'

Und coomed his hoompoogs ofer Schmit,
Till Max saidt, ' *Nun— ich gehe mit!* ' [1]

All in de finster mitternocht,[2]
Vhen oder folk in shleep vas lock't,
Down in de Wolfsschlucht,[3] Kass tid try
His tyfel-strikes und Hexerei.[4]

Mit skools und pones he mate a ring,
De howls und spooks[5] pegin to sing,
Und all de tyfels oonder-croundt
Coom preakin' loose und rooshin' roundt.

[1] ' Well, then, now I will go along with you !'
[2] In the dark midnight.
[3] The wolf's glen.
[4] Hexerei. Witchcraft, sorcery.
[5] Spook : *Ger.* Spuk, spectre, hobgoblin.

Denn Maxerl cooms along : says he,

' Mein Gott ! vot dings ish dis I see !

I dinks de fery tyfel und all

Moost help to make dem magic ball.

' I vish dat I had *nix cum raus,*[1]

Und shtaid mineself in bett to house.'

' *Hilf, Zamiel!* ' cried Kass ; ' you whelp—

You red[2] Dootch tyfel—coom und help !'

Denn up dere coomed a tredfull shtorm,

De todtengrips[3] aroundt tid schvarm ;

---

[1] I wish I had *not come out.*

[2] Red devil.   The Germans speak of the devil as being *red*, just as we talk about his being so black ; thus their phrases, ' Rother Teufel,' red devil ; ' Roth, wie der Teufel,' red as the devil.

[3] Todtengrips : *Ger.*   Todtengerippe, skeleton.

De howl joomped oop und flopt his vings,
Und toorned his het like efery dings.[1]

Oop droo de croundt here coomed a pot
Mit leadt, und dings to make de shot ;
Und hœllisch fire in grimson plaze,
Und awful schmells like Schweitzer kase.[2]

Agross de scene a pine-shtick flew,
Mit seferal jail-pirds fastened to ;
Six treadtful jail-pirds, mit deir vings
Tied to de shticks mit magic shtrings.

---

[1] 'Efery-dings,' as a ready-made convenient comparison, is almost in as high favour with Anglo-Germans as the favourite ' Teufel.'

[2] Swiss cheese, almost as powerful in its smell as the Limburger Käse, alluded to in a foot-note on p. 19, Part I., of this work.

All troo de air, all in a row,
Die wilde Jagd[1] *vas seen to go ;*
De hounts und deer all mate of pone,
Und hoonted py a skilleton.

Dere coomed de tredful shpecdre pig
Who shpitten' fire, afay tid dig ;
Und fiery drocks[2] und tyfel-shnake
A-scootin'[3] droo de air tid preak.

Boot Kass, he tidn't mindt dem alls,
Boot casted out de pullet balls ;

[1] The wild hunter of German legends. See **Bürger's**
' Wild Huntsman.'
[2] Drocks: *Ger.* Drachen, dragons.
[3] Scooting—vulgar pronunciation of 'skating.' A very
common Americanism, implying a noiseless sliding move-
ment, as when a man desires to leave without other persons
being aware of the fact.

Six vas to go ash he vouldt like,
De sevent' moost for de tyfel shtrike.

Ad last, oopon de drial tay,
De gals coom'd roundt so nice und gay,
Und denn dey goed und maked a tantz,
Und singed apout de *Jungfernkranz.*[1]

Und denn der Hertzhog—dat's de Duke—
Cooms down und dinks he'll dake a look :
'Young mans,' to Maxerl denn says he,
'Shoost shoot dem dove oopon dat dree !'

Denn Maxerl pointed mit de bix,
'Potzblitz!' says he, 'dat dove I'll fix !'

[1] Song of the bridal orange wreath. Chorus from Weber's opera, ' Der Freischütz.'

He fired his rifle at de *Taub'*,[1]

When Kass roll'd ofer in de *Staub*

De pride she falled too in de doost,

De gals dey cried—de men dey coossed :

Der Hertzhog says, ' Id's fery glear

Dat dere ash peen some tyfels here !

' Und Max has shot mit tyfels-blei ![3]

Pfui !— die verflucte Hexerei ![4]

O Maximilian ! O Du

Gehst nit mit rechten Dingen zu !'[5]

[1] Taube : *Ger.*   Dove, pigeon.

[2] Staube : *Ger.*   Dust.

[3] Devil's lead, devil's bullet.

[4] ' Fie ! out upon such sorcery !

[5] ' Oh, Maximilian ! Oh, you—have not done this by proper means !'—'not acted in a straight-forward manner.'

But denn a hermits coomed in late;
Says he, ' I'll fix¹ dese dings foost-rate :'
Und tell'd der Hertzhog dat young men
Will raise der Tyfel now und denn.

De Duke forgif'd de Kaspar dann,
Und mate of him ein Yægersmann,
Vhat shoodts mit bixen goon und pfeil,²
Und talks apout de Waidmannsheil.³

Und denn de pride she coomed to life,
Und cot to pe de Maxerl's wife ;
Denn all de beoples cried ' Hoorah !
Das ist recht brav !⁴ und hopsasa !'

¹ 'Fix.' To manage, to settle, to dispose of a matter; a
favourite Americanism.
² A huntsman who shoots with muskets, guns, and arrows.
³ Sportsmanship, hunting.
⁴ ' This is capital !—and so hurrah !'

HANS BREITMANN IN POLITICS.

I. THE NOMINATION.

VHEN ash de Var vas ober, und Beace her
shnow-vite vings
Vas vafin' o'er de coondry (in shpodts) like
efery dings;
Und heroes vere revardtet, de beople all pegan
To say 'tvas shame dat nodings vas done for
Breitemann.

No man wised[1] how id vas shtartedt, or vhere
    der fore-shlog[2] came,
Boot dey schveared it vas a sin dereto, a
    purnin' shame :
Dere is Schnitzerl in de Gustorm-House-
    potzblitz![3] can dis dings pe !—
Und Breitmann he haf nodings : vot sights is
    dis to see !

' Nod de virst ret cendt[4] for Breitmann ! ish *dis*
    do pe de gry

---

[1] ' Wissen ;' *Ger.* To know, to understand.

[2] ' Fore-shlog,' rough English, for 'Vorschlag;' *Ger.* The
'proposal,' or, in this instance, the 'first mention.'

[3] ' Potzblitz,' a German burlesque oath, meaning, if anything, 'nameless lightnings!' It has, also, a slanting reference to our English 'possible' ('is it possible?'), in the
mouth of a blundering German.

[4] ' Red cent,' the smallest American copper coin in circu-

On de man dat sacked de repels und trinked
dem high und dry?
By meine Seel'[1] I shvears id, und vot's more,
I deglares it's drue,
He vonce gleaned oudt a down in half an oor,
und shtripped id strumpf[2] und shoe.

'He vas shoost like Koenig Etzel, of whom
de shdory dell,
Der Hun who go for[3] de Romans und vollop
dem so vell,

lation, in contradistinction to the 'white cent,' made of
nickel.

[1] 'Seele;' *Ger.* Soul,—upon my soul!

[2] 'Strumpf;' *Ger.* Stocking.

[3] 'To go for,' to rush at with the fiercest determination.
Originated by Western hunters and trappers, who, being
robbed by Indians, would, emphatically, 'go for' them. It
is also used by American politicians in the sense of 'to be in
favour of,' as 'I go for peace with England.'

Only dis, dat dey say no crass vouldt crow
    vhere Etzel's horse had trot,
Und I really pelief vere Breitmann go de
    hops shpring in de shpot.' [1]

Iv vunce you tie a dtog loose, dere ish more
    soon geds aroundt,
Und venn dis vas shtartedt on Breitmann id
    was *rings herum* [2] be-foundt;
Dough *vhy* he *moost* hafe somedings vas nod
    by no means glear,

[1] In allusion, of course, to Breitmann's love of Lager-beer. The *Louisville Journal* said of Southern generals slain in battle, that their places of interment would be known by the corn and rye growths, consequent upon the quantity of whisky they had drunk ; which the *New York Atlas* capped by saying that the whisky was so bad in the North, that the Union-generals' burial-places would be recognised by the blasting of the vegetation for miles around.

[2] All round about.

Nor tid id, like Paulus' confersion, on de snap [1]
to all abbear!

Und, in facdt, Belthazar Bumchen saidt he
couldtent nicht [2] blainly see
Vy a veller for gadderin' riches shood dus re-
vartedt pe :
Der Breitmann own drei Houser, mit a wein-
handler in a stohr,
Dazu ein Lager-Wirthschaft,[3] und sonst wo
—somedings more.

---

[1] 'Schnapp ;' *Ger.* A slap, or snap, hence this phrase 'at
the first glance.'

[2] 'Nicht ;' *Ger.* Not, a double negation as a vulgar
strengthening of the emphasis.

[3] *I. e.,* 'Der Breitmann owns drei Häuser mit a Wein-
handler in a store (shop), dazu ein Lager-Wirthschaft, und
sonst wo,' German-English for ' Breitmann owns three houses,

Dis plasted[1] plackguard none-sense ve couldn't
  py no means shtand,
From a narrow-mineted shvine's kopf,[2] of our
  nople gaptain crand :
Sooch low, goarse, betty *bornirtheit*[3] a shentle-
  man deplores ;

with a wine-shop, together with a Lagerbeer-house, and other
property.'

[1] The English reader will have very little difficulty in re-
cognising this familiar piece of English profanity.   It is not
to be met with in the long list of recognised American oaths,
and is invariably used in that country to denote that a
Britisher is present.   This, and a still more sanguinary expression, are generally supposed to constitute the main cha-
racteristics of Cockney speech ; thus Artemus Ward makes
the Colonel of the Seventy Onesters in Canada, say : —
'What? Impossible ! It kannot be ! Blarst my hize, sir,
did I understan you to say that you was actooally goin into
the presents of his Royal Iniss ? '

[2] Shwine's kopf; *Ger.* Pig-headed fellow.

[3] Bornirtheit, an equivalent for shallow-brained contracted
genius.

So ve called him *verfluchter Hundsfoot,*[1] und
shmysed [2] him out of toors.

So ve all dissolfed [3] dat Breitmann shouldt haf
    a nomination
To go to de Legisladoor,[4] to make some dings
    off de nation ;
Mit de helb of a Connedigut[5] man, in whom
    we haf great hobes,

[1] 'Verfluchter Hundsfott,' *Ger.* a dirty miserable scoundrel, a rascal.

[2] 'Schmeissen ;' *Ger.* To fling, altho' *histed* would be the American vulgar expression.

[3] Resolved. The Americans are continually holding meetings, political or otherwise, at which the various 'Resolutions' are introduced by the formula : — 'It is resolved that,' &c.

[4] *The* Legislature, in the States of the Republic, is the Lower House of each State, or the House of Representatives, branch of the Congress.

[5] A Connecticut man.

Who hat shange his boledics fivdeen dimes,

und derefore knew de robes.[1]

'To know the ropes,' from ship language, to be fully
informed.

D ENN for our Insdructions Comedy de
ding was protocollirt [1]
By Docktor Emsig Grubler, who in Jena vonce
studiret ; [2]
Und for Breitmann his insdrugtions de Comedy tid say
Dat de All out-going from de Ones vash die
first Morál Idée.

[1] Placed upon record
[2] 'Studiren,' *Ger.* To study.

Und de segondt crate Morál Idée dat into
　　him ve rings [1]

Vas dat government for efery man moost
　　alfays do efery dings ;

Und die next Idée do vitch his mindt esbe-
　　cially ve gall,

Ish to do mitout a Bresident und no govern-
　　ment ad all.

Und die fourt' Idée ve vish der Hans vouldt
　　alfays keeb in fiew

Ish to cooldifate die Peaudifool,[2] likevise de
　　Goot und Drue ;

[1] 'To ring' facts into a person, is to beat them into him
by continual application; to keep 'ding-donging' at him with
such persistency that he must take notice.

[2] This sounds very much like a burlesque of the grandi-

Und de form of dis oopright-hood in proctise
  to present,
He moosht get our liddle pills all bassed, mitout id's gostin' a cent.

Und der fift' Idée—ash learnin' ish de cratest
  ding on eart,
Und ash Shoopider der Vater to Minerfa gife
  ge-birt'[1]—
Ve peg dat Breitmann oonto oos all pooplic
  tockuments

loquent title of N. P. Willis' '*Home Journal, for the Culti-
vation of the Beautiful and the Sublime.*' In America many
educated persons are very fond of aiming at perfection in
life ; indeed, communities of individuals have been formed
for this purpose, but the societies, to use a colloquialism,
invariably ' come to grief ' after a short duration.
  [1] Geburt, *Ger.* Birth.

Vich he can grap or shteal vill sendt—franked[1]
—mit his gompliments.

Die sechste crate Morál Idée—since id fery
vell ish known

Dat mind ish de resooldt of food, ash der
Moleschott has shown,[2]

---

[1] 'Franked,' letters and packets pass free through the U. S. Post Office if they bear the mark, seal, or token of a Member of Congress, given at Washington, while Congress is in Session. Hence industrious 'Congressers,'—as the vulgar term these gentlemen in office,—make good use of the privilege in keeping their constituents well supplied with Congressional documents,—similar to our Blue Books. It is very doubtful if the bulk of our Government publications ever found their way to the butter-shops—as they certainly do now—if Members of Parliament were allowed to circulate them free through the post as in the United States. It should be stated that as the office of local postmaster is a Government appointment in that country, this official is generally one of the most active politicians for his party in the neighbourhood of his office.

[2] Moleschott, an eminent German chemist, at present professor at Turin

Und ash mind ish de highest form of Gott, as
    in Fichte [1] dot' abbear—
He moost alfays go mit de barty dat go [2] for
    lager-bier.

Now ash all dese insdrugdions vere showed to
    Misder Twine,
De Yangee boledician, he say dey vere fery
    vine :
Dey vere pesser ash goot,[3] und almosdt nice—
    ' a tarnal tall consarn ; '

[1] The works of Fichte have been translated and published in America ; and it is said that in the neighbourhood
of Boston there are many converts to his teachings.

[2] ' To go for,' to be in favour of, an Americanism much
affected by political and other public speakers, thus :—' Will
Mr. Greeley say that he or any other citizen has the right to
oppose "the country ?" We say *go* for your country, right or
wrong ! '—*Gospel Banner.*

    ' Pesser ash goot,' 'better than good,' a form of ex-

Boot dey haf some liddle trawpacks, und in
fagdt weren't worth a dern.[1]

Boot yed, mit our bermission, if de shentle-
mans allow—
Here all der Shermans in de room dake off
dere hats und pow—
He vouldt gif our honored ganditate some
nodions of his own,
Hafing managed some elegdions mit sook-
cess, as vell vas known.

Let him plow id all his *own* vay, he'd pet as
sure as born,

pression as general amongst the Americans mingling with
Germans, as amongst the latter themselves.

[1] See in the *Biglow Papers*, how the Yankee deludes

Dat our mann vouldt not coom oud of der
liddle endt der horn,[1]
Mīt his good *proad* Sherman shoulders—dis
maket oos laugh, py shink !
So de Comedy shtart for Breitmann's—*Nota
bene*—after a trink !;[2]

himself that he escapes the consequences by mispronouncing
an oath.   Very amusing are these attempts to cheat the Devil.

[1] Imagining a pigmy imprisoned in a cow's horn, he
would display little sense by trying to squeeze himself along
out by the tapering extremity in preference to leaving by the
expanding way to the large mouth.   To come out of 'the
little end of the horn' is a common Americanism in the sense
of a failure, an unfortunate ending, a bad speculation.

[2] Among politicians, very little is done in America un·
less preluded by a libation.

III. MR. TWINE EXPLAINS BEING 'SOUND UPON THE GOOSE.'[1]

D ERE, in his crate corved oaken shtuhl der Breitemann sot he :

[1] The following is a different origin of the phrase, 'Sound upon the goose.' One of the U. S. flags displays a spread eagle in the union, with the stripes on the field, which the irreverent have likened to a goose broiling on a corner of a gridiron. Hence, faithful to the American eagle, would be paraphrased 'Sound on *the* goose.'

Bartlett, in his 'Dictionary of Americanisms,' says,

He lookt shoost like de shiant in de Kinder
hishdorie;[1]
Und pefore him on de tische, vas—vhere man
alfays voundt it—

'GOOSE. "To be *sound on the goose,*" or "*all right on the
goose,*" is a South-western phrase, meaning to be orthodox
on the slavery question, *i.e.* pro-slavery. Although it only
got into general use during the recent Kansas troubles, I am
not able to give its origin.'
  'The border ruffians held a secret meeting in Leaven-
'worth, and appointed themselves a vigilance committee.
'All persons who could not answer "*All right on the goose,*"
'according to their definition of right, were searched, kept
'under guard, and threatened with death.'—*Mrs. Robinson's
Kansas*, p. 252.
  A poetical writer in the 'Providence Journal,' in speaking
of the claims of a candidate for the office of Mayor, says :—

  'To seek for political flaws is no use,
    His opponents will find he is *sound on the goose.*
                                    June 18, 1857.

[1] 'Kinder-historie :' *Ger.* Children's story-books.

Dwelf inges of goot lager, mit a Bœmisch glass [1] aroundt it.

De foorst vordt dat der Breitmann shpoke he
maked no sbeech or sign :
De nexd remark vas, ' *Zapfet aus !* '[2] de dird
vas, ' *Schenket ein !* '[2]
Vhen in coomed liddle Gottlieb und Trina mit
a shtock
Of allerbeste Markgraefler wein—dazu dwelf
glaeser Bock.[3]

* A Bohemian glass.
[2] 'Zapfen aus,' *Ger*. Tap the cask ; and 'Schenken ein,'
' Pour into the glasses.' The Germans put a whole cask on
the table ; tap it (anzapfen)—then fill the glasses (schenken
ein), and then drink.
[3] ' The very best Markgraefler wine, with a dozen glasses
of Bock bier (Buck beer, a favourite brewing).

Denn Misder Twine deglare dat he vash happy
to denounce

Dat as Copdain Breitmann suited oos eg-
sockdly do an ounce,

He vas ged de nomination, and need nod
more eckshblain :

Der Breitmann dink in silence and denn roar
aloudt, CHAMPAGNE![1]

Den Mishder Twine, while trinken wein, mitwhiles vent on do say,

Dat long insdruckdions in dis age vere nod de
dime of tay ;

Und de only ding der Breitmann need to pe
of any use

[1] The Americans were early in taking up the Paris 'fast'
fashion of 'champagning' on grand occasions.

Vas shoost to dell to efery mans he's *soundt oopon der coose.*

Und ash dis liddle frase berhops vas nod do
    oos bekannt,[1]
He dakes de liberdy to make dat ve shall
    oondershtandt,[2]
Und vouldt dell a leedle shdory vitch dook
    blace pefore de Vars :
Here der Breitmann nod to Trina, und she
    bass aroundt cigars.

'Id ish a longe dime, now here, in Bennsyl-
    fanian's Shtate,

[1] Known.
[2] *Ger.* Verstehen, to understand ; unterstehen, to dare.
Many Germans in England and America mix the two words,
under (*Engl.*), stehen (*Ger.*); verstanden (participle).

K

All in der down of Horrisburg[1] dere rosed a
    vierce depate,
'Tween vamilies mit gooses, und dose vhere
    none vere foundt—
If gooses might, by common law, go squan-
    derin' aroundt?

'Dose who vere nod pe-gifted mit gooses, und
    vere poor,
All shvear de law forbid dis crime, py shings
    und cerdain sure;
But de goose-holders teklare a goose greadt
    liberdy tid need,

Harrisburgh, the capital of the State of Pennsylvania, and
the seat of the State Legislature, is situated about 100 miles
N. W. of Philadelphia.

Und to pen dem oop vas gruel, und a mosdt
uon-Christian teed.

'Und denn anoder barty idself tid soon re-
feal,
Of arisdograts who kepd no coose, pecause
'tvas not shendeel :
Tey tid not vish de splodderin geese shouldt
on deir pafemends [1] bass,
So dey shoined de anti-goosers, or de oonder
lower glass !' [2]

[1] The pavement in America is the gravel, or other kind
of footway before the doors of dwelling-houses.

[2] Breitmann's Yankee friend seems to have got bewildered
in the writings of some recent English political econo-
mists who delight in explanations of the lower-middle class,
with such variations as the ' higher-middle,' the ' middle-
lower,' the ' higher-lower,' &c. &c.

Here Breitmann led his schdeam [1] out : ' Dis
    shdory goes to show
Dat in poledicks, ash lager, *virtus in medio.*
De drecks ish ad de pottom—de skoom floads
    high inteed ;
Boot daas bier ish in de mittle, says an goot
    old Sherman lied. [2]

' Und shoost apout elegdion-dimes de scoom
    und drecks, ve see,
Have a pully [3] Wahl-verwandtschaft, [4] or elec-
    tion-sympathie.'

' To let one's steam out,' in the sense of giving vent to
one's feelings or opinions, is a phrase quite as common in
America as it is here.

  [2] ' Lied,' *Ger.* Song, hymn.

  [3] ' Bully,' fine, large, powerful ; an Americanism explained
at pages 24 and 64 of the *First Part* of this work.

  [4] Coming together by a common liking,—in other words,

'Dis ish very vine,' says Misder Twine, 'vot
here you indrotuce :
Mit your bermission I'll grack on mit my
shdory of de coose.

'A gandertate for sheriff de coose-beholders
run,
Who shvear de coose de noblest dings vot
valk peneat' de sun ;
For de cooses safe de Capidol in Rome long
dimes ago,
Und Horrisburg need safin' mighty pad, ash
all do know.[1]

a family gathering or meeting, voting for one's own kin-
dred.   Elective affinity.

[1] Harrisburgh, as the seat of the State Legislature, en-
joys a not very enviable reputation in the newspapers pub-

'Acainsd dis mighdy Goose-man anoder veller
    rose
Who keepedt himself ungommon shtill ven
    oders gome to plows;
Und if any ax how 'tvas he shtoodt, his
    vriends vould vink so loose,
Und visper ash dey dapped deir nose : ' He's
    soundt oopon de coose !

' He's O. K.¹ oopon de soobject : shoost pet

l·shed in other parts of Pennsylvania.   The terms ' Jobbery '
and 'Corruption ' are almost as well known there as in
Washington.
   ¹ ' O. K.' had its origin in the following circumstances.
Previous to a Presidential Election, the political parties in
large towns have processions to parade their strength.   In
New York, about the year 1845, one district was distin-
guished by a banner bearing this strange device : ' *The
Fourth Ward*, O. K.'   Next day everybody who had seen
the sight neglected business to compare notes with others as

your pile [1] on dat :
On dis bartik'ler quesdion he indends to coot
it fat.'

to its signification. At last, the public bewilderment rose to
such a height that one individual, more curious than the rest,
resolved to beard the author-sphynx in her den. He went to
the secretary of 'the 4th Ward Democratic Committee,' who,
surprised at such ignorance, loftily exclaimed: 'The Old
Fourth having got tired of stale mottoes, has for novelty's
sake, adopted a commercial one from our leading merchants.
Don't they say, when they would affirm that a clerk can be
implicitly relied upon to produce a balance on the right side
"OLL KORRECT !"' The banner-painter acted up to his in-
structions in the way we have seen.

In 1868, 'the *Great Vance*' attached 'O. K.' to the chorus
of his so called 'great' song 'Walking in the Zoo,' and thus
London is delighted by an obscure New Yorker's ignorance ;
—'great *O. K.'s* from little acorns grow.'

It is a curious fact that the telegraph clerks in England
and America employ the letters 'O. K.,' when they send a
telegram that a message has been received *Oll Korrect.*

[1] Formerly 'To bet one's pile,' was to stake all the gold
and notes heaped up before a gambler on the table ; now the
phrase means to stake one's entire wealth.

So de veller cot elegtded pefore de beople
foundt
On *vitch* site of der coose it vas he shtick so
awful soundt.

'Dis shdory's all I haf to dell,' says Misder
Hiram Twine ;
'Und I advise Herr Breitmann shoost to
vight id on dis line.' [1]
De volk who of dese boledics would oder shap-
ders read,
Moost waiten for de segondt pardt of dis here
Breitmann's Lied.

[1] President Grant.   'We will fight it out *on this line* if it
takes all summer.'

PIET BREITMANN IN CINCINNATI.

[NOTE. *Already Hans Breitmann's popularity has pro-*
duced imitations. The following comes from the West, and is
supposed to be tne production of his son Peter, who has emi-
grated as far as Cincinnati to open a Lager-Beer 'Saloon.'
If Peter's liquor was no better than his verse, the 'bhoys' who
sacked the establishment ought all to have been pardoned to a
man. He is a poor hand at rhyming after his father.]

PIET[1] BREITMANN Zinzinnatty,
Mooch honored mit his schoise,
Ven he oopened dere a pier-saloon,
To show Gambrinus' joys,[2]

[1] 'Pete,' for Peter : *German.*

[2] 'Gambrinus' is the German Roi d'Yvetot, the patron
of beer-drinkers : usually represented as a jolly, round-bellied,
middle-aged king, in the dress of 1300, or so, astride of a
beer-keg, and lifting a frothing beer-mug.

Und I dell him mit a letter
To let us vellers hear
How de poy vas gettin' on,
Und gettin' off de pier.

Hochst[1] glad to see Hans' schreibart[2]
Like ash your beshtesht schwanke![3]
I dips mein quill in lager,
Mein Vater,[4] for my danke!
Dey's nice poys in dish city,
For, ven I opened toor,
Dey roosh in py de tozens
Mit halloh und hurrah!

[1] Highly, greatly.   [2] Writing.
[3] Merry tale.   The Breitmann family were beginning to be proud of the head's literary celebrity.
[4] My father.

Und ven I say, 'who makes de pay
For dis crand cellarbrate ?'
By tam, dey say, und vink at me :
'You puts him on de schlate !'[1]

I dells 'em I don't keep schiefer,[2]
Ven dey lift deir haar, undt gry :
'Here, Yakey, dake my beafer![3]
Send out a schlate to puy!'
I like to aggommodate
(Dere'sh no brincipal in dese tings !),[4]

[1] Scores, to be easily removed when paid, are written on slates, hung in American country, and even city, taverns.
[2] 'Schiefer :' *Ger.* Slate.
[3] 'Yakey,' familiarly for Jacob : Jacob being for Germans in America what John is for Chinamen in California, or for Englishmen in the Crimea to the Turkish allies. 'Take my beaver' for 'take my hat.'
[4] A German liquor-dealer of Cincinnati failed to recover

So I puys a schlate, more proad like a schkate
Und puts down all de gals [1] prings.

Recht quick de schlate alretty
Pees full, geheim be-pressed, [2]
Und dey dells me I, te petter
' Vill my tam Tootch het mit de rest !'
Pooty bimeby in a leedle

damages on suing some riotous customers, as his evidence
could not make the court distinguish the ringleader. The
Justice of the Peace remarked that it was hard on the publi
cans, as it seemed to be a rule that no principal, or instigator
in these bar-room brawls could ever be singled out. The
prosecutor, afraid of the rowdies' vengeance, prudently (ever
in his letter to Hans Breitmann) sweetens his complaint with
declarations that his boisterous guests were ' nice boys ' never
theless.

[1] Peter had waitresses to serve his patrons, as is the usua
custom in beer-gardens.

[2] ' Closely pressed,' the figures he had to put down.

Dey makes smash !—mein bar gits vits !'
Trinks mein pottles unt knockt der teufel
Out mein spiegel mit ice-spitz' !²
How I vash mad ! I 'd radder
Haf so mooch ash I vash mad
(Put dere 'sh no brincipal in dese tings !)—
Dey'se nice poys, efery lad.

Dey called me tam Tootch hiker ;³
I shtand in silent gontempt,

¹ 'To give fits,' *Am.*, is to produce that state in the victim
which will make him apparently have been under the effects
of strong convulsions ; to utterly ' use him up.'

² 'Spiegel :' *Ger.* Mirror. Ice-spitze : the ice-pick, which,
in bar-rooms, is a necessary tool in summer, where refrigerating
beverages are in full demand.

³ ' Hiker,' a word popular among the lower orders for a
German, the Dutch being, as in this case, superfluous ; it is
merely an English corruption of 'haken :' *Ger.* A hook.
The rag-pickers of New York and other eastern sea-ports, are

Und shouted, 'Bolice !' ven de barty,
　Like de tream Herr Faustus treamt,
Raced [1] my gals oop der staircase,
　Frow'd de winder clean throo dem outdoors!
Oopset der shtove oopon der zink, [2]
　Und it burnt right throo der floors !
But dey say dis is Geschaft, [3]
　Dere 's no brincipal here!

mostly Germans ; their only implement is an iron hook ; hence, they are 'hookers.' Therefore ' hooker,' or ' hiker,' becomes a generic title of contempt for the whole German-American population.　Our English ' to hook,' ' to steal,' comes from this implement in the hands of beggars and sturdy vagabonds of Henry the Eighth's time.

　[1] ' To race,' *active :* as ' to walk a horse ;' ' to lead or drive a horse out at a walking pace.'

　[2] The stove being set in the room itself, the wooden flooring would take fire if not shielded, which is done by a sheet of tin, or zinc.

　[3] ' Geschaft,' business. This damage to Peter was ' all in

Dey *pees* nice poys—but warum—

Wherevor vater mein pier?

Vat vor tid dey vill mit nails

My match-pox on der shelf,

Und ven dey plowedt der gas out,

It vash der Teufel's self;

Vor, drying to light, I schraped

Die paint, und de tables wreckedt,

Und schrammt¹ holes in der nachtbar's wall,

He threaten process-rechte !²

Dish ish nicht der Stil,³ you look !

Dere's *some* brincipal in dese tings !

the way of his business,' since the publican must expect
drunken frolics.

¹ 'Schrammen,' to scratch.

² An action at law.

³ In 1869, a song of the music-halls has again revived
'That's the Style' as a popular saying, or cry, of the streets.

I schlachte[1] mein schlate, und I gifs

NO TICK nimmermehr,[2] by shings!

---

[1] Schlachten, to butcher ; he smashed the slate, he slaughtered it, in the midst of his excitement.

[2] Nevermore.

PRINTED BY W. W. HEAD AND MARK, FLEET LANE, OLD BAILEY, E.C.

2.

www.ingramcontent.com/pod-product-compliance
Lightning Source LLC
Chambersburg PA
CBHW020554270326
41927CB00006B/832